T0123431

CRIMINALS

ALSO BY ROBERT ANTHONY SIEGEL

All the Money in the World
All Will Be Revealed

CRIMINALS

My Family's Life on Both Sides of the Law

ROBERT ANTHONY SIEGEL

COUNTERPOINT
Berkeley, California

Criminals

First hardcover edition: 2018

This book is a work of memoir. The events, locales, and people described are as the author remembers them.

"Milk" is reprinted by permission of Ecco, an imprint of HarperCollins publishers.

Library of Congress Cataloging-in-Publication Data
Names: Siegel, Robert Anthony, author.
Title: Criminals : my family's life on both sides of the law /
Robert Anthony Siegel.
Description: Berkeley, CA : Counterpoint Press, [2018]
Identifiers: LCCN 2017057587 | ISBN 9781640090378
Subjects: LCSH: Siegel, Robert Anthony. | Siegel, Robert Anthony—Family. |
Authors, American—20th century—Biography.
Classification: LCC PS3569.I3822 Z46 2018 | DDC 813/.54 [B]—dc23
LC record available at https://lccn.loc.gov/2017057587

Paperback ISBN: 978-1-64009-227-3

Cover designed by Donna Cheng
Book designed by Jordan Koluch

COUNTERPOINT
2560 Ninth Street, Suite 318
Berkeley, CA 94710
www.counterpointpress.com

Printed in the United States of America

For the chain gang

MILK

I flew into New York
and the season
changed
a giant burr
something hot was moving
through the City
that I knew
so well. On the
plane though it was
white and stormy
faceless
I saw the sun
& remembered the warning
in the kitchen
of all places
in which I was
informed my wax
would melt
no one had gone high
around me,
where's the fear
I asked the
Sun. The birds
are out there
in their scattered
cheep. The people
in New York
like a tiny chain
gang are connected
in their
knowing
and their saving
one another. The
morning trucks
growl. Oh
save me from
knowing myself
if inside
I only melt.

—Eileen Myles

CONTENTS

CRIMINALS

Memory Loop

AT THE AGE OF six, I struck a deal with the school bus driver: on the afternoon trip home, he would let me off at the stop where the mean kids got on. I wanted to avoid them, but that was only part of it: I wanted to be outside, in the world. I wanted to walk home.

I can't imagine why he agreed. Maybe it was one less stop to make toward the end of his run, or maybe he really believed that I could navigate the city on my own and saw no reason to cage me up in the dark and rattling bus. At very least, he must have assumed that I knew my address.

I stepped off and walked to the corner. It had never occurred to me that not knowing where I lived might be a problem. My building had a green awning and a brass door and a red carpet leading to the elevator. The windows in our living room were covered by heavy green drapes that for some reason I associated with my mother. I would wrap myself up in them, or slip past them and stand in the narrow space between the fabric and the window, looking down at the cars and the pedestrians and feeling the intense mystery of her love for me.

This is a way of saying that I could feel my home's presence among the thousands of other buildings that made up the city, could feel a path leading there as if through my own body. The light changed, and I began to walk.

Everything around me was in motion, too. People sped in all directions, plunging in and out of stores, leaping into phone booths, yelling into the black phone receivers with great passion. I couldn't believe that all this happened, invisible, while I was in school. That the world went on when I wasn't there to see.

That's when I recognized the blue sign above Klein's department store, where my mother had bought me a suit in the husky department, a tan three-piece number with a vest and bell-bottom pants. That suit was so elegant—I knew I was going right, that I would find my way home. I knew it, too, when I passed the Chock Full O' Nuts, which had chromium stools lined up at the counter like giant silver mushrooms.

I passed Union Square and headed up Park Avenue, where the buildings were tall and the sidewalks always in shadow. I felt the temperature drop. I felt a lateness that had something to do with yearning. So much time had passed since the bus, since my parents in the morning. I stopped at an office building that had a small glass display case by the entrance containing maybe a dozen books with covers so ugly they were strangely beautiful. It had never occurred to me that books were made somewhere, but now I had stumbled on the place, and it felt momentous. I read the titles out loud, under my breath, as if they were the directions I'd been waiting for. Then I pressed my hand against the building's dark granite façade and felt the cold stored up there, and I knew I had to hurry.

THREE YEARS LATER, WHEN I was nine, my parents decided to buy an apartment in a building a short walk away. The movers were coming to get the furniture and the boxes while I was at school; after school, I would walk to the new apartment instead of the old one; my parents would be there, waiting for me.

I kept putting that thought in my head and then instantly forgetting it. I had spent my entire life in the old apartment, and couldn't quite imagine us as existing completely independent of its surroundings. My mother was, to me, the woman on the couch by the heavy green drapes; my father was the man standing in the entrance to the little kitchen, taking up the whole doorway. Those spaces gave them their shapes, their lights and shadows, mixed with the touch of their hands and the sound of their laughter to make them into the people I knew as my parents.

Walking home, I kept reminding myself that I was going to the new apartment, not the old, but the idea kept falling out of my head. There were all the familiar sights to make me forget: Fourteenth Street lined with bargain clothing stores, the racks spilling out the door and onto the sidewalk; Union Square, full of light; the shadows of Park Avenue South. I became completely absorbed in the flow of the city around me, propelled onward by the hidden current, and when I turned the last corner and came to my block what I saw in front of me was not the new building but the old, its green awning with white letters, its little flower beds with their tiny white flowers. I felt pleasure and relief, all the feelings of home, and yet I knew that I'd made a mistake: this wasn't my home anymore.

It was then that I realized I had no idea how to get to the new apartment. I couldn't quite visualize the route, and I didn't know the address or the phone number or even what street it was on. It hadn't occurred to me to learn those things.

I felt a surge of panic, but at the same time a wave of exhaustion so intense my eyes began closing. My love for my parents appeared as something infinitely sad and beautiful, a form of nostalgia. What I pictured were the granite ledges, the iron grates, and the empty dark basement entrances of the cityscape, all the lonely, useless places: those were me without them.

Not knowing what else to do, I opened the door to the lobby and walked to the elevator, keeping my head down so I wouldn't be spotted. Up until that morning, the doormen had seemed like friendly extensions of the building itself, but I was a trespasser now, slipping like a ghost into the elevator, pressing the button marked 12, the number that to my mind had always stood for *us*.

When the elevator opened, everything in the hallway was exactly the same as it had always been: the same speckled wallpaper, the same little wooden table. I walked across the carpet, pressed my hands to our door, and felt my parents' presence, vibrating on the other side. When

I knocked, my mother would open up and I would be home: that was a wish so beautiful it was going to turn out true. All I had to do was make a fist and rap on the door with my knuckles, and my alternate, imaginary world would become real and let me in.

Instead, I turned around and took the elevator downstairs, stepped out into the street again, and began walking. The journey was haphazard, a question of feel, in part because it took me past the drugstore on Third Avenue, which marked the outer perimeter of where I was used to going by myself. And so, the relief when I saw that big brown building, a sort of terraced ziggurat. I had no key, didn't know the apartment number, but when I entered the lobby, my father was standing there with some boxes, looking at me without surprise, as if he'd always expected me to show up.

THIRTY YEARS LATER, MY parents were still living there, in that building. My father was dying of Alzheimer's, and I stopped by one afternoon to take him outside for some sunshine. He had been a trial lawyer, the old-fashioned kind that quoted Shakespeare to his juries, but language was leaving him behind now, like a fading memory. He'd forgotten how to read, and simple speech was difficult, so we just sat on a bench in silence.

"When I was a kid," he said, finally, "the sky was blue and I would run. I would run very fast."

I looked up. The sky was indeed very blue, luminous, endless. "I wish we could run away together," I told him, thinking about his illness, the way it had walled us in on all four sides.

"Yes," he said, nodding. "We would run home."

CRIMINALS

In the winter of 1972, our entire family went to Rome with a client named Basil so my father could take care of a small legal task for him. Basil was a marijuana dealer, and my father was a criminal defense attorney, but the legal matter was commercial and took only a few days. Then we drove around the country looking at artistic treasures, which my mother believed essential to our development. "A truly educated person needs to spend an afternoon standing in front of a Titian as the light changes," she told me. "He needs to feel the Sistine Chapel floating over his head."

My mother had wanted to become an English professor, but her parents pushed her into law school, which she loathed. Since getting married, she had quit the law and devoted herself to a strenuous regimen of culture—museums, theater, classical music—everything she saw as defining the larger world beyond her native Brooklyn.

Brooklyn was parochial, she told us, claustrophobic, terminally stupid. "Just look at your father's family," she said. "They all live together on that one little dead-end street, clustered together as if in a shtetl. They never go to Manhattan. They don't read books. And they don't like it when anyone else does either."

We were going to be different. I felt her urgency as *our* urgency. I remember walking with her into the Uffizi in Florence, seeing the walls covered from top to bottom in dark old paintings in gilt frames, and feeling my heart sink with fear: it was just way, way too much. I was ten years old. My brother David, who was nine, and my sister, Perrin, who was four, had gone with my father in search of a café, and part of me wished I were with them, eating cannoli.

"Isn't this incredible?" my mother whispered. "We're in one of the greatest museums in the world. And we're going to see absolutely everything."

I never said no to her, because I was afraid of her disappointment: a flicker of her eye, a look of judgment, and then boredom. Becoming a sort of tiny bewildered art aficionado was the way I tried to earn her love. Back in New York, we went to MoMA and the Whitney to see Pollocks and Motherwells, huge paintings that seemed to vibrate against the massive white walls. I'd already decided that I wanted to become an artist, but what I really wanted, on some unconscious level, was to become a *painting*, so my mother could look at me with the same intense expression she had when we stood in front of a Rothko or a De Kooning: rapt, open, wondering.

In Italy, I did indeed stare up at the Sistine Chapel's frescoed ceiling, far, far above my head in the afternoon semidark, felt myself pulled upward, as if I were rising above the crush of other tourists, communing with Michelangelo. I walked around the city with my father, amazed by the way the street would curve and suddenly we were in front of something out of a dream: a giant Neptune blowing a conch shell, or a bronze child riding a porpoise, laughing. I remember going to the Coliseum at night and finding out that it wasn't really a building so much as a rank darkness filled with feral cats slinking among the stones, eating from aluminum pans of pasta. The world was just like art, unpredictable and mysterious, made to surprise.

I remember us all marching into Basil's hotel room one night to watch him play the guitar. Tall and thin, he seemed to twine around himself as he plucked the strings, and then he stopped and reached up and casually removed his hair—a wig. His own hair was tied up in a bun on the top of his head. He shook it out till it went all the way down his back.

I knew what a wig was, of course, just hadn't ever seen one; in the moment, it looked as if he were magically changing his hair from short to long. But because no one else said anything I kept quiet, too, until my mother explained later, in our own room. "He wears the wig so the Italian police won't hassle him."

"Why would they do that?"

"They don't like people with long hair—counterculture people."

And then she veered off in a new direction, because she tended to narrate her thoughts without filter, in a sort of associative stream that never took my age or experience into account. "Basil believes that psychedelics like LSD are the next step in human evolution, that they will lead humanity to new levels of understanding. I'm not completely sure he's right, but he certainly makes a compelling argument. What do you think?"

Of course I had no idea what to think. What I felt was jealous of Basil, and uncertain about what my mother wanted—what would make her love me. Looking back, I don't believe she had any real interest in psychedelics or the doors of perception. Rather, I think she was uneasy about the possibility that our family's situation might be exactly as it seemed: that the clients might simply be criminals, and my father's profession just a way to make money. Money wouldn't distinguish us from limited people. She wanted to think we were involved with something intellectual or artistic or at very least bohemian and *interesting*, something that proved we belonged to the world of freedom and beauty beyond Brooklyn.

And so the opposition between the clients and the law became confused for me in some subtle way with the opposition between my mother's ruling categories. The clients were art. The police and prosecutors were art haters, philistines. We were art lovers, and my father's job was protecting art against the stupid and the cruel. That odd take on the situation became an essential part of me, a part of my love for my parents and my belief in their wonderfulness—so much so that I couldn't help feeling its beautiful reality even once I grew older and saw it wasn't true.

NINE YEARS LATER, IN the summer of 1981, I learned that my father was under investigation for a long list of crimes, including drug trafficking and weapons possession. I came to the news late, as I'd just gotten back from a junior year abroad in Tokyo, where I'd spent my time watching Noh plays and visiting temples—carrying on my mother's work, essentially, though now it had become my work, too.

My brother David was the one who told me what had happened, one very hot night as we walked down Fourteenth Street. There were a lot of people milling around the sidewalk, somebody with a boom box every few feet, a mishmash of clashing salsa stations. David described how a client by the name of Jay had gotten arrested for planting a bomb that had blown off the hands of a cop, a member of the bomb squad sent to diffuse it. He explained how Jay had turned out to be a fugitive, wanted under a different name, and how our father was suddenly removed from the case by the judge. The DEA raided his office and took all his records, and he had to hire a lawyer to get them back, who then convinced him to go in and answer questions under oath. "They asked about guns, cocaine, orgies, like he was some kind of drug lord."

I felt strange, light-headed, as if I'd been spinning in circles. I could almost see the two of us walking down the street, as if I were outside myself, hovering. "I don't get it, why?" I asked.

"Jay's talking his way into a deal. The more incredible he makes it, the more they eat it up."

We were at the Hudson by then, standing at the edge of the river, looking out at the water, black and oily. "Why didn't anyone tell me?" I asked, finally. The only letters I'd gotten were from our mother, short notes about things like buying socks or getting stuck in traffic on the crosstown bus—well-intentioned lies, I saw now.

"Mom wouldn't let us. She didn't want to ruin your experience," he said.

"That's incredibly mixed-up."

"Exactly."

When we got back to the apartment, our parents were sitting at the dining room table, clearly waiting for us, and I realized that they had deputized David to tell me what they couldn't bear to tell me themselves. My father's face, always exquisitely sensitive, now registered the most intense and delicate shame. His father had been a bus driver, unemployed throughout the Great Depression, and he was haunted by the idea of parental failure. All his effort had gone into being the opposite: a guy with money who bought us things, whatever we wanted, as soon as we wanted it.

"It's a bit of a mess," he said. "I acknowledge that. But it's going to be all right."

"I know it will," I said, eager to believe.

And then with my mother sitting beside him, he took me through the facts of the case in a very lawyerly way, as if I were a member of the jury.

What I learned was that Jay's real name was in fact the utterly fake-sounding Ralph Rogers. My father had first met him 1968, when Rogers was a teenage runaway, selling dime bags on the street; he would come by the office, and my father would buy him lunch.

"Your father was always feeding runaways," my mother cut in to say. "His office was a kind of hangout for the lost."

My father represented Rogers on a case in 1971, until Rogers jumped bail and went underground. Clients did that sometimes, panicked about the prospect of prison. The very strange thing was that Rogers returned a few years later—just walked into the office sporting a new name. And my father didn't recognize him.

"Why would he?" said my mother. "His practice was growing. He had hundreds of clients by then."

My father nodded, his eyes big and earnest. "I was so busy, I couldn't remember my own name."

"So busy he didn't know what day it was," my mother added.

Anyway, there was no reason to connect Ralph Rogers with Jay.

Rogers had been a skinny street kid, but Jay was an adult, clean-cut and dressed in expensive clothes—nothing obviously counterculture about him. He had lots of money and bragged about big deals involving tons of marijuana transported by boat and plane.

"Why did he come back?" I asked.

My father gave one of his supremely eloquent shrugs. "How should I know? And why does it even matter? He hung around the office a bit. We went to lunch sometimes. But I never did any legal work for him."

"Then you didn't do anything wrong," I said.

"Exactly."

And yet the story was just so odd, even as I sat there exercising total suspension of disbelief. Why would Rogers contact him again, given the risk of being found out? And how could my father not recognize him?

"What happens next?" I asked.

"They will figure out that all of this is bullshit, and then everything will be okay."

His face was his courtroom face, carefully matter-of-fact, but his eyes were frightened, and I felt such a rush of helplessness that I had to get up and go to my room and shut the door. Standing at the window, I tried to hold myself together by listing all the reasons he was obviously right. Somebody in the prosecutor's office would certainly see that this was bullshit. Somebody would see that we were intelligent, that we had been to Paris and Rome, that I had lived in Tokyo without ever resorting to English. And then I remembered that afternoon in the Sistine Chapel when I stood in the middle of a crowd and felt myself pulled upward into the ornate ceiling—the feeling that I was actually rising. I wanted to rise up now, hover over whatever was happening to us, the terrible things they were saying about us, the fear in my chest. But I didn't know how.

Looking for witnesses to back up Rogers's assertions, investigators began calling my father's other clients. It was the equivalent of telling them to get a new lawyer, which of course they all did, as fast as they could: all the clients who supposedly loved us so much, all of them gone over the course of a single summer.

My father had always been prone to what my parents called *depression.* They didn't mean that in the medicalized sense current today but as a kind of exasperating character flaw that was a by-product of his genius as a lawyer—a trade-off they considered annoying but unavoidable. Now he slid into the deepest depression I had ever seen, dozing most of the day on the couch, roaming the apartment at night. He had a history of binge eating when he was upset, and this became the binge of all binges, a tsunami of hunger that emptied the house of food, down to the very last bacon bit. At times his eyes looked shocked and frightened, as if someone else had control of his body. At other times his expression was determined and purposeful, as if he were carrying out some dark and inscrutable vengeance on the world. I stumbled on him scooping mayonnaise straight out of the jar with a pack of hot dog buns. I watched him chew bullion cubes. Once I walked into the kitchen and found him standing in the dark, crunching uncooked spaghetti out of the box.

Over the years, I had learned how to fake a certain detachment at times like this, though in fact I seethed with anger underneath, as if he were pushing the dry pasta down my throat instead of his own. He was hurting himself; he was hurting *us.* "I can boil some water for you," I said.

"Not necessary."

"Are you feeling okay?"

He closed the box and put it on the counter. "Excellent, actually." He was in nothing but his boxers—already so bloated that his clothes didn't fit him anymore. His eyes had the small, fiery intensity of the terminally sleepless. And then he dropped his voice, as if the next part were top secret. "I got a call this afternoon from someone with a message from Jay." He paused, his fingers reaching out for the spaghetti box and then withdrawing again. "Jay says I've got nothing to worry about. He'll never testify against me."

"And you believe that?"

"Of course I do."

Later that night, David and I went for another of our long walks, in which we engaged in recursive analyses of the legal situation and circular debates about what to do before it was too late. It was clear to both of us that our parents were in denial, but we had no idea how to open their eyes. David believed our current lawyer wasn't tough enough.

"We need a pit bull," he said, "someone who will make them pay for every inch of ground until they decide it's just not worth it anymore."

The problem was that our father was obviously way too fragile for that kind of approach, and though we talked big, so were we—soft, passive, terrified, resentful of the fact that we still felt like children. We sat on a bench outside a neighborhood playground, trying to imagine a way around our lack of toughness.

"Remember the Angels?" asked David, sounding wistful. "They were really tough."

Our father had represented Hells Angels for years, and I had watched them in court: huge, silent men who sat at the defense table without emotion, no matter which way the case was going.

"But they're psychopathic murderers," I said, as if that explained it.

"Yeah, I guess you're right."

Of course I can see now that this discussion contained its own form of denial. It allowed us to go on believing that we had made no mistakes, that there was nothing wrong in living with criminals in our strangely starstruck way.

But in early September, right before my departure for school, I came downstairs one afternoon and found my father standing with the phone in his hand, a weird expression on his face. "I just got a call from an old client."

"Yeah?"

"And it was just such a strange conversation. He kept asking—he seemed to be trying to get me to say—"

"What?"

He sat down on the couch, looking as if some terrible realization were dawning on him, negating everything he knew about the world. "I had the feeling he was recording me."

A NEIGHBOR ONCE SAID to my father, "I don't know how you can represent somebody you know to be guilty. They just go back on the street and do it again, hitting old ladies on the head and taking their pocketbooks, or selling drugs to schoolkids."

I was nine or ten, and I remember the man's smug outrage, and how it made me shrink back, ashamed and confused. Later, I would learn how to bury those feelings in a complicated smugness of my own, modeled on my mother's idea of our specialness, our superior culture. But in the moment, I felt the man's implication fully: we were little more than criminals ourselves.

My father didn't seem at all put out by this. He explained that the criminal justice system is designed to be adversarial, and that it is the defense lawyer's job to advocate for his client, not decide who is guilty or innocent. "All I do is make the best argument. It's the jury that decides."

"So they get off on technicalities."

"Well, it's called due process." And then suddenly he drew himself up and began to recite something that sounded like a poem: "I didn't say anything when they came for the drug addict, because I wasn't a drug addict. I didn't say anything when they came for the streetwalker, because I wasn't a streetwalker." Even outside the courtroom, he was a performer, something of a ham, always launching into a snippet of verse or a long, stagey story. Now his chin was up, his eyes moist with emotion. "I didn't say anything when they came for the thief, because I wasn't a thief. So there was nobody left when they came for me . . ."

Of course, I had no idea that he had appropriated those lines from Martin Niemöller, the German theologian who survived Dachau—appropriated them and then retrofitted them to our very peculiar situation. But standing beside him, I felt their odd force, a strange rush of need. I wanted somebody like him to protect me, and in some reflexive twist of consciousness, I think he wanted somebody like him to protect him, too. As much as anything, it was an expression of longing.

To put that another way, my father's profession was a container in which we placed everything most urgent and troubling in our lives: our desire to be loved, our fear of disaster, our confusion over who was helping whom and what might make us okay.

There was an abject, helpless quality to his need for his clients. He needed their need for him; it gave him a sense of purpose and a place in the world. When they didn't call, he would lie down on the couch and gaze up at the ceiling, or stare at a magazine without turning the page. He would eat dinner in silence, examining the label on the ketchup bottle. "Make him get up and take you somewhere," my mother would tell me, and he and I would slouch off to the park or the zoo or a department store, where he would wander off and lose me. I spent a great deal of time with policemen and zookeepers looking for him, or standing at information desks while his name went out over the PA system. At some point I got smart and took to grabbing on to his coattail, letting him pull me forward while I trotted behind. He was going nowhere in particular, just walking very fast with his head down, deep in thought.

My mother once saw me clutching the hem of his jacket as we got ready to leave a restaurant. "How utterly brilliant," she said. "I should do that, too."

Is it any surprise that everything about him was luminous and beautiful to me? That I would sometimes just sit and watch him as he lay on the couch, wondering what he was thinking and what I could do to save us? I tried to tag along wherever he went, even to the bank or the supermarket or the drugstore, to make sure he was okay. But none of that ever satisfied my longing for him, because even when we were together I missed him, as if he weren't actually there.

The only thing that shook him back to life was a call from a client. When the phone rang, he would jump off the couch and grab it, hoping it was one of them.

This is later, when I was in high school, but I remember him leaping up to get the phone, and then throwing on some clothes. Together we drove to a beachside restaurant on Long Island—a ridiculously long drive—where a client by the name of Stephen Pfeiffer was waiting for us in jeans and no shirt. It was a weekend at the very tail end of summer, and we sat at a wooden picnic table on the restaurant patio, the wind surprisingly cold off the water, the light beautiful.

"Stan, you were right about that thing," said Pfeiffer.

My father nodded. He looked relieved to be out of the house, alive again. "So it turned out okay?" he asked.

"Yeah, I just stayed clear."

"Wise move."

I was never sure what that sort of veiled language was about, especially because at other times they could be totally open and unfiltered, but I was used to it, almost as if it were a ritual of belonging, the language of a club at which I could never be more than a guest.

The two men smiled and turned their faces up to the sun, sharing a moment of genuine companionship. Pfeiffer was, like Rogers, a runaway, a street kid grown to adulthood in the marijuana trade. A few years earlier, my father had gotten him off a seemingly unwinnable weapons-possession case, a magic victory that had sealed their connection.

Pfeiffer turned to me. "Your dad is a legal genius, you know."

Of course I knew; I'd seen it with my own eyes: my father standing in a courtroom with marble walls and high ceilings and tall thin cathedral windows, the judge and jury taking in his every word, laughing at his jokes, *believing*.

"I do love winning," said my father.

"Fuck the government," said Pfeiffer, smiling. He sounded as if he were saying, *Isn't this a beautiful day! What great weather!*

My father nodded. "Amen, brother."

In the fall, the prosecution started paring back, trying to focus in on charges that might have enough substance to stand up in court. The drug running, the weapons, the orgies all disappeared, never to be mentioned again. It is possible that they had been meant only as a kind of negotiating tool, a way to exert some pressure on us. Now there was just a couple of relatively modest accusations left on the table. It turned out, for one, that my father had in fact done a single small piece of work for Rogers, the lease on a store in Manhattan. And the name on the lease was Jay.

"The paralegal drew that up, not me," said my father. "I never touched it. In any case, I only knew him as Jay. There was no reason for me to think he was anyone else. I told them that at the very beginning."

Maybe a different sort of family might have been relieved, even grateful, that he wasn't at risk for a big prison sentence anymore. But we weren't that family. We had become obsessed with our blamelessness, our innocence, our goodness; the sheer plausibility of the new charges made them painful to us, and we denied them even harder. I was at school by then, but I would call David to rant for hours about the injustice of it all. He would call me with complicated conspiracy theories. Class was just a place to sit and obsess till I could get to a phone with new points to make, or more exactly, new versions of old points. The space inside my head was completely filled with our drama, and at the center of our drama were the prosecutors and their incomprehensible stupidity, their willful blindness. How could reasonably intelligent people fail to see my father's goodness, our fundamental innocence?

And then one night in my dorm room, sitting at my desk by the window, I caught a fleeting glimpse of a different picture. It was almost as if I'd turned my head and caught the same scene from a slightly different angle. In this other picture, my father most definitely recognized that Jay was Ralph Rogers: there was no way he couldn't have recognized him. They may have acknowledged it openly, or they may have left it unspoken. My father may have thought that it didn't really matter, since Rogers wasn't looking for a lawyer, just someone to talk to—which was fine, because my father could never have enough people to laugh at his jokes, to drive around town with him on his perpetual search for snacks, to call him up in the middle of the night to interrupt his insomniac's vigil.

I saw this all very dimly, and then I looked away and forgot it completely. My memory had been wiped clean of something I shouldn't have ever seen.

When I got home for Thanksgiving, my father was different. No longer eerily upbeat, he had pretty much stopped talking. If you spoke to him, he would glance at you ruefully and light a cigarette. Of course, he refused to answer the phone, believing it was tapped. At my mother's insistence, the festivities went on around him, without in any way acknowledging the weirdness of the moment. We had a couple of relatives and some family friends over, everyone forced to step around my father, who in my memory, at least, never got up from the TV.

I had no words for what was happening and therefore no way to think about it. All my energy went into pretending that we were the same and I wasn't afraid. The result was a strange sense of unreality, as if my life were a stage set and I was playing myself rather than *being* myself. I didn't ask my parents any questions because I didn't want to hear anything that would throw off my performance—anything that would trip me up and reveal that I was terrified.

My father and I spoke only once the entire vacation, when he came up to me with a yellow legal pad in his hand. "You're interested in writing," he said.

"Well, yeah, sort of." I'd taken a couple of poetry workshops in school.

"I've written something."

He sat down and read me the opening of a scene about a man who puts the barrel of a shotgun in his mouth. I remember it as carefully written, in a close third-person point of view, running something like this:

He placed the barrel in his mouth, and for the first time in years he felt like a human being, in control of his destiny. He realized now that this was what he had been longing for all that time, a sense of control. He would decide his fate, no one else.

"What do you think?" he asked.

"It's well written," I said, recalling that it was very possible there was a shotgun in the house, a gift from a grateful client, which he used to keep under his bed. He'd taken it out and shown it to me once, years earlier, and I remembered its heavy dark strangeness, its air of power and menace.

"All I have to do is finish it," he said.

"Don't rush. You could write a whole novel if you wanted to."

He put down the pad. "Nobody would believe it."

To this day, I am deeply ashamed that I didn't tell anyone about what he had written, given that it obviously sounded like a suicide threat. I know that I understood the seriousness of what had happened: I'd gotten through the moment holding my breath, as if I were walking across a plank laid over a deep crevasse. But once the moment was gone, I didn't even check under his bed to see if the shotgun was still there; I simply locked the whole episode away, out of reach. And when he offered me a ride to the airport the following afternoon, I was just glad that I wouldn't have to take a cab.

That was a mistake. By the time we were on the Grand Central Parkway, he was going much, much faster than the rest of traffic, casually drifting from lane to lane, oblivious of the other cars, which were doing everything they could to avoid us. I must have looked scared, because he stared at me with an oddly bemused expression, speaking as if he and I were both other people, the words so fundamentally *not his* that to this day they don't exist for me and I can't remember them. What I do remember is shrinking back against the passenger-side door, wondering if I should risk grabbing for the wheel before we flipped and crashed.

And then he smiled at me from a seemingly infinite distance. "Don't worry, I'm back," he said. It seemed to be true: the car straightened out and started to slow.

"Where'd you go?" My voice came out squeaky and small.

He gave a smug laugh, as if this were a ridiculous question.

At the terminal we enacted a sort of normalcy, hugging and saying goodbye at the curb as if nothing unusual had happened, and then I walked inside on shaky legs and down the long corridor to my gate and got on my flight, my mind circling the absurd thought that my father had, perhaps, just experimented with the idea of killing us both. That was impossible, of course. The truth, I knew, was that he loved me. He was the one who had stayed up with me all night when I got a bottle of whiskey from the liquor cabinet and drank myself sick in high school; he was the one who drove me up to college for freshman orientation and cried when it was time to leave, covering his face and running to the car so I wouldn't see. The smell of his aftershave and the touch of his big hand on my shoulder were among the most essential facts of my life, running through my earliest memories back to the point when memory itself started. Maybe I had filled some sort of weird caretaker's role—I was dimly aware of that possibility. We would drive through the city for hours together when he was depressed, from Katz's for pastrami to Junior's for cheesecake and the Hong Fat Company for roast pork, red as candy apples. On those nights, we ate till eating felt daring, like jumping from the high diving board, as if it were an expression of exuberance rather than fear. But I didn't regret any of that: those hours had healed my own loneliness, too.

How could that strange, blurry car ride to the airport, the things he'd said to me then, so foreign that I couldn't even remember them, outweigh the evidence of twenty years of love? By the time I reached my dorm room, the episode in the car had started to feel distant and dreamlike, almost as if it were a story I'd made up, a figment of my imagination rather than an actual event. As with his fictionalized suicide note, it never occurred to me that I might tell anyone. My silence didn't feel like secret-keeping so much as space-making, a kind of careful pushing away, as if I were closing a window, inserting a pane of glass between me and what was happening to us.

In the weeks that followed, I continued to go through the motions of being myself, a student in his last year of college. The kids around me were going on job interviews, applying for graduate schools, but I didn't know what to do, or whom to ask for direction. I'd call home, and my mother would say that everything was fine, my father in the living room watching TV, but she didn't seem to have the energy to ask about me or my plans and I never pressed her. I was having trouble sleeping: I would sleep for a couple of hours and then wake up in a panic, gasping for air, my heart skittering in my chest. It felt as if I were back in the car on the way to the airport, sliding between lanes. Afterward, I would sit at my desk, drinking bourbon and trying to read the eleventh-century *Tale of Genji* in classical Japanese, with two different dictionaries open alongside. The sentences were unbelievably long and complicated, like vines entangling an ancient palace, and I would follow each strand as best as I could, trying to see the wonders hidden underneath, even as the bourbon made the print blur and my head spin. Really, it was another attempt to circle back to that moment in the Sistine Chapel when I stared up at the ceiling and felt myself rise above the confusion of who we were, artists or criminals or just plain fools. Up there, it wouldn't matter anymore: we would be safe, and I would be able to sleep.

My father would have had a pretty good chance at trial if he'd fired his lawyer and hired a pit bull, as David wanted. Rogers would have looked awful under cross-examination. But there was no money left, and even if there had been, my father was too fragile to testify on the stand. Just being around him you had a sense of his weirdness, even when he remained absolutely silent: the pouchy red eyes, the strange, angry look on his face. A plea bargain was fast and cheap, and we were certain that nobody was going to send a fifty-five-year-old man to prison on charges like these. The judge noted that there seemed to be no clear motive for the crime, no financial incentive, no reason other than an "excessive need to serve." Nevertheless, when the time came, he sentenced my father to three months. Ralph Rogers went free, no jail time at all.

I was back in Japan when this happened, studying on a scholarship at the University of Tokyo, and I got the news in a single brief letter from my mother, probably written in great sorrow: just a quick recitation of the facts, free of the sugarcoating you really long for when it's not offered. At the end, in a sort of postscript, she added that my father didn't want me to write to him; he wanted to be left alone.

That request may have been about nothing beyond his sense of failure, but at the time, it felt like an accusation. It felt as if he was saying that I had failed to take care of him as I was supposed to, as I had when I was a little boy and we had driven around the city at night when he couldn't sleep. My face stung, as if he had slapped me—and then I caught myself and methodically folded up the letter, slipped it into the garbage, and went about unpacking my groceries. Later, as the weeks passed, I made a conscious effort not to think about him or the prison camp in Danbury,

Connecticut, where he was now living—until one night when the phone woke me, and I picked up the receiver.

I still slept badly, but every couple of weeks the exhaustion would accumulate and I'd fall into an incredibly deep slumber like this one, so deep I could barely speak.

"Sorry," he said. "It's not easy to get to a phone in here."

"No, no, I was up." I struggled to put words together, afraid that if I didn't talk, he might slip away and never call back. "How are you?"

"Fine, fine, listen, I've got a friend here who wants to start a business exporting hair to Japan."

"Hair?"

"Yeah, human hair, to make wigs."

He explained that real human hair is the most lifelike thing you can use to make a wig, and that Japanese wig makers can't get enough to meet demand. "The market's there, the problem is the import licenses, and that's when I thought of you."

"Sure, I can help," I said, starting to worry about who this friend was and what I might be getting into. For one dreamlike moment I imagined his friend murdering people for their hair. "Whatever you need."

"That's great," he said, and then fell silent for a little while. "How have you been?"

"Good," I said, not knowing how to begin.

"Good, good, listen, there's a line for the phone so I better go," he said. "I'll call again soon."

Afterward, I sat drinking tea as the window turned blue, feeling his voice continue to vibrate inside my body, the sound of the past, of home.

Many years later, my father would tell me that he had no choice but to talk about wigs because his friend, who was paying for the call, was standing beside him; really, he'd just wanted to hear my voice, and this was the only way he could afford to do it. But there was no way for me to know that, and I was left feeling as if he were trying to draw me into a shady scheme. He then added to my contradictory sense of injury by never calling again.

Instead, my mother came for a visit with an extremely large suitcase that took up an entire corner of my one-room apartment, and we went about the weird project of seeing the sights as if we were ordinary tourists and not humiliated, heartbroken criminals, teetering on the edge of bankruptcy. Museums, castles, temples, shrines: we followed a strict and rigorous schedule, dutifully reading all wall plaques and examining every object, down to the smallest scrap of calligraphy, until it was closing time and we were forced to return home, too exhausted to be afraid of the future.

One afternoon, we took the train to an old area of town called Yanaka and wandered in and out of the temple graveyards, rising above our sense of failure and grievance long enough to become entranced by the great beauty of the place. One graveyard in particular held us for a long time because it was full of hundreds of small Buddha statues that had been broken into fragments; someone had painstakingly collected the pieces of each figure and grouped them on the ground in neat rows, as if planning to come back and glue them together. The effect was otherworldly: the broken-up baby-size statues laid out like skeletons at an archeological dig, their calm Buddha faces lost in dreams . . . For a moment I forgot about being doomed, and just breathed. And then I looked over at my mother and saw that she held one of the heads in her hands and was staring into its eyes.

"What are you doing?" I said. "Put that back."

"Your father would love this."

"Put it back right now," I hissed.

"It's just lying there. It doesn't belong to anyone."

I never argued with my mother, because I knew from long experience that I was bound to lose, but temple-robbing was a line I did not want to cross. Instantly, intuitively, I felt that it would destroy my connection to Japan.

She began stuffing the Buddha head in her purse.

And then a very angry voice yelled in Japanese, "Hey, you there, stop that!"

I looked up and saw a monk standing on the veranda of the temple building, staring at us. He'd evidently been there for some time, watching.

"Go home!" he roared in Japanese. "Get out of here!"

"Put it back," I whispered to my mother, who meekly complied. I bowed low to the monk.

"Get out!" he screamed.

My mother and I walked quickly together, as fast as we could, gripping one another's arm for comfort, heads bowed in shame, out the gate and down the street, as the monk bellowed, "Get out of here! Get out! Out!"

The act of taking that Buddha head was so small and so gratuitous that it seemed, paradoxically, to cut deep into who we were. On the train home, we didn't look at each other, and we never mentioned what had happened.

My mother left soon after, and I fell into a period of depression. The sight of her trying to push that stone face with its forgiving smile into her purse kept playing in my mind, along with the roaring of the monk, telling us to get out. Anger at her and pity for her got so mixed up inside me that I couldn't lift myself from the tatami, and I spent a couple of days just staring out into the building's tiny courtyard, with its potted plants and rake and shovel and metal barrel for burning leaves, acknowledging what I'd always secretly known: that Japan was just a beautiful dream, a fantasy in which I imagined shedding an older version of myself for a newer, less conflicted, one. If only my mother hadn't come to visit, bringing her extra burden of sorrow, I told myself; if only the monk hadn't been standing there, watching; if only I were less like my parents, less awful, maybe then I could still believe.

LIFE IN NEW YORK was different when I got back. My mother had found work as an attorney for the City's child welfare agency; every morning, she put on a suit with big shoulders as if strapping on armor, packed her briefcase with files, and marched out the door to the subway, looking determined and a little frightened. David had gotten a job as a veterinary lab technician at the Animal Medical Center and was living in an apartment on Sixteenth Street he sublet from a former client of my father's (though the man would come back eventually and throw him out in the middle of the night, and he would end up moving to Brooklyn). My sister, Perrin, was at a progressive boarding school in Massachusetts, learning how to paint pictures and take care of a cow.

My father was home by then, driving a Meals on Wheels truck for a synagogue on the Lower East Side as part of his court-mandated community service, but otherwise showing none of the earnest desire to rejoin society expected of an ex-con. When not driving the van, he sat in front of the TV, eating and smoking, a strange sort of grief on his face.

I needed advice, but he was in no shape to give any, so I went for long walks to get out of the apartment, touring the scenes of my youth, nostalgic for a time when we browsed used books at the Strand and watched samurai films at the Regency on Broadway and argued with great passion about the best place to get linguini in white sauce or Hunan beef. Back then, my only goal in life was to be an art lover in the strange way my parents and I defined that endeavor, encompassing the clients and their eccentric undertakings and everything counterculture and *interesting*. Insofar as I ever thought of an adult occupation, it was stirringly vague: painter, philosopher, novelist. I had no idea what to do next, no idea how grown-ups generally put a life together so that they don't look shameful to other people. I had a vague sense that a job of some kind might be in order, but I'd never had one and didn't know how to go about looking. And then one afternoon, down by the World Trade Center, I saw a group of Japanese tourists getting out of a big tour bus, gathering around a tiny Japanese woman holding a little red flag on a long pole: a tour guide. She started to march across the vast concrete plaza and they followed behind, like chicks following a hen.

I can do that, I told myself.

And I did. I got a job with a Japanese travel company working as a Japanese-speaking tour guide, taking groups around the city. I would rumble around New York in a gigantic bus, interpreting the world for them through a microphone. Look to your left, I would say in Japanese, and watch the bright, open faces swivel left. There is the Empire State Building, 103 floors, 1,250 feet tall if you include the antenna. It takes 1,872 steps to get to the top. Look to the right. There is Macy's Department Store, the same as in the movie *Miracle on 34th Street*, starring Maureen O'Hara and John Payne, which won three Oscars in 1947.

I stood at the front of the bus, one hand gripping the microphone, my other arm wrapped around a pole, acting as if I were an authority, a source of truth. But of course what I felt was the exact opposite, the complete emptiness of everything I knew of life. My old view of the world made no sense to me anymore, and yet I wasn't quite rid of it, either, because I had nothing to replace it with. It floated behind everything, like a double exposure—like a reflection in the bus window.

Back at home, I would take off my suit and tie and look in on my father. He talked infrequently, but when he did it was an acidic monologue about the prison camp and the prison guards, whom he called *screws*—a term that sounded so retro that I thought maybe he was making it all up from old Cagney movies. Except that occasionally he would retreat to a darkened room and weep.

And then one day I saw him answer the phone, listen for a while in silence, and then put the receiver back in its cradle—pressing down with his hand, as if trying to close the lid of a box that didn't want to shut.

"This phone is tapped," he whispered to me.

I, too, had noticed some problems with the connection, but the idea that it was tapped didn't make a lot of sense, especially considering that everything was over now, his case finished, his time served. When I told him that, he gazed at me condescendingly, pitying my naïveté. And in that moment, I had a dim, half-formed thought that he might actually be crazy.

He got up very quietly and went to his room. A little later, he came out combed and dressed and left the apartment to see Stephen Pfeiffer, the man we'd once met for lunch at the beach, the only client with whom he'd remained close. When he returned late that night, he was carrying something new, an old-fashioned vinyl flight bag, which he hid under the orange shag carpet in David's old bedroom, creating a hump that was impossible to miss. Then he sat down in an easy chair to watch it, brooding.

The next day, David came by after work and took me aside. "That bag is full of money."

"How do you know?"

"I took it out when he went to the bathroom."

Money had a new kind of urgency for us. Once it had been the thing my father needed more and more of so he could spend it more and more quickly without actually feeling any better. Now it was something we didn't have enough of and needed for the rent and the electric bill.

"How much?" I asked him.

"I don't know. It's packed full."

A couple of days passed and I did nothing, just watched my father watch the lump in the carpet, until finally I couldn't stand it anymore. "What are you going to do?" I asked him one night, as he sat smoking in his chair.

It was a strange feeling, asking a question after all the missed opportunities over the last few years. It felt like stepping out onto a high ledge, with the same sense of a fall about to happen. His face turned furious, agonized, and I realized that he had been waiting for me to ask him this.

"Why should I tell *you*?" he asked.

"Don't you think I deserve to know?"

"No, I don't."

But of course he told me anyway; having it both ways was always the family style. He was planning to drive up to Buffalo, he said, where Stephen Pfeiffer lived. Pfeiffer knew someone there who would sell him a false passport he could use to cross into Canada and then fly to a third country, where he could start a new life under a new identity.

"But why?" I asked.

He told me that the government was angry he'd gotten off so lightly the first time and was now plotting to frame him for something really big.

"The case is over. You've served your time."

"It's not over for *them*," he said. But of course what he meant was that it wasn't over for *him*, that it never would be.

I could feel my face growing fragile, as if it were made of glass. "Where are you going to go?" I asked.

He lit another cigarette, looking cagey. "Wouldn't you like to know."

We fell into silence. I looked around at all the objects I'd grown up with: the shag carpet, the bunk bed, the big chest of drawers, the nubby armchair in which my father sat—all those familiar things which made the world feel knowable, stable. They seemed to be tilting now, like the deck of a ship in heavy seas. But my father just stared out the window at the cityscape beyond, imagining his journey to safety.

That journey would, in fact, remain imaginary. He would sit in that chair for days, smoking and watching TV, staring out the window, trying to gain the strength to pull the flight bag out from under the rug and leave for Buffalo. Eventually, he would give up his vigil and wander the house, as if testing an alternative wish, to stay. In the process he would spend the money till it was gone, the bag squashed flat: vast quantities of Peruvian take-out chicken, Italian shoes with monk straps, a silver bracelet. Some months later, he would begin seeing a psychiatrist, who would start him on medication, and in a couple of years, he would actually win his law license back and practice law again, in the same courthouse where he was once sentenced to prison—practice with modest, self-deprecating humor and a newfound sense of caution.

But on that first evening, there was no way for me to know how it would finally end, and I stumbled out to my own room, almost drunk on fear. I had to get to the Hotel Edison on West Forty-Seventh Street to lead a nightlife tour: dinner at a steak house, then drinks at a Folies Bergère–themed nightclub where we would watch women dance around in plumes. Just pulling on my suit and tying my tie seemed to take forever, and I had trouble finding my flag, but I got out the door and onto the subway, and then suddenly I was standing in the Edison's worn lobby, the tourists slowly gathering around me, shy and tentative.

"I have the great honor of serving as your tour guide tonight," I said in Japanese, bowing deeply. "Of course, I beg your forgiveness for being American. I will nevertheless try my best. Please rest assured that you can depend on me."

I raised my flag, and they followed me out the front doors to the sidewalk and onto the bus. The pneumatic doors closed, and we took off down Forty-Seventh Street, then turned on Eighth Avenue and headed uptown.

I stood at the front of the bus with the microphone, one arm wrapped around a pole for balance. The city I'd grown up in was moving past, a shiny patent leather darkness full of beautiful lights. I looked over the seats and saw the tourists gazing back at me with their expectant, trusting eyes, and I knew that I needed to speak. This was the point where I normally introduced myself and explained the schedule, the places we would be going, and the things we would be doing. But the words wouldn't come, even as my heart beat faster. What I really wanted to tell them was that I didn't know if my father would be there when I got home. That I had no idea where we were going.

Stan, Darling

WHEN I WAS GROWING up, our living room was dominated by a six-foot-high picture of a comic-strip panel in the style of Roy Lichtenstein. The painting depicts a man and a woman kissing in tight close-up, dialogue bubbles floating above their heads. The man says, "I'm a criminal attorney, honey! I make a fabulous salary and can afford to buy you champagne and caviar every night of the week!"

The woman replies, "Stan, Darling, don't let me wake up and find out this has been a dream . . ."

That scenario drew from life: my father was indeed a criminal defense attorney named Stanley, my mother blonde, just like the woman in the picture. She had commissioned the painting for his birthday from a client of his, an artist who had gotten busted for drugs. But visitors to the house didn't know that last bit of information. They would look at the painting and say, "Hey, isn't that by what's-his-name?"

"Roy Lichtenstein?"

"Yeah, that guy in the museums."

We would smile with great modesty, letting the mistake vibrate around us, uncorrected.

In quiet moments, with nobody around, I would sit on the couch and stare at the painting, trying to figure out what it said about us. Mom and

Dad were characters in a piece of art, real but more than real, so fabulous that they could spoof themselves in a fake Lichtenstein and be even more fabulous for it. Except we didn't tell anyone that it was a fake. Neither did we claim that it was real. The painting was a little like what my father did in court, spinning stories for the jury that were beautiful possibilities, wishes that lived in the spaces between the facts. And yet the painting had truth inside it, too—I could feel it there, in the man and the woman, the kiss. I would try to make sense of the dialogue bubble in the next panel, only a sliver of which was visible, reading it as if it were a crossword that needed to be filled in: *It, dre, sha, res, lives, bec, goin . . . It isn't a dream, my love. We shall live the rest of our lives together, because we are going to be happy.*

I'M A CRIMINAL ATTORNEY, HONEY! I MAKE A WONDERFUL SALARY AND I CAN AFFORD TO BUY YOU CAVIAR AND CHAMPAGNE EVERY NIGHT IN THE WEEK!
STAN DARLING, DON'T LET ME WAKE UP AND FIND OUT THIS HAS BEEN A DREAM...

GOURMETS

WE WERE THE KIND of family that ate out a lot, because home was too rancorous and depressing, and we tended to be a little nicer to each other in public. We went to the Hong Fat Company on Mott Street, where the roast pork was a succulent red I've seen only in a Rothko canvas, and to the Automat, with its banks of little windows that made you feel as if the building itself knew what you wanted to eat. We went to cheesy places like Luchow's and posh places like Peter Luger. We wanted to find the perfect example of crabs in black bean sauce, of kugel with raisins; we wanted to be filled and transported, understood and made content. Typically, we just ate too much and left dazed. And yet we never stopped believing in the transformative power of food, even as we understood, deep down, that it was an illusion. "I'll have one of those," my father would say to the waiter, pointing to an insanely large dessert, "and a dose of insulin." It was his standard joke, and it always got wary laughter because he was scarily heavy.

We spent a lot of time discussing my father's weight, usually over dinner. The conceit was that he was the only one with an eating problem because he was the only one who was obese—the rest of us were just a little husky. "Your father eats to soothe his anxieties," my mother explained one night in Sammy's Rumanian, drizzling clear chicken fat from a dispenser onto a big hunk of rye.

He nodded, chewing. "I eat because I'm depressed."

"That's the problem," said my mother. "Food should be a form of sensual enjoyment, not a tranquilizer."

My mother liked to contrast herself with my father whenever possible: he was crazy and she was sane; he was a slob and she was cultured; he watched TV and she went to the theater, the symphony, and the ballet. In the arena of food this pattern played out through a very simple opposition: he liked steak and she preferred haute cuisine, usually French and expensive. She kept trying to get him to take us to Lutèce or another of the great New York restaurants, but he resisted—and not solely because of the money. Dinner was a fraught endeavor for him, so loaded with desire that he couldn't compromise very much. He needed to eat, not dine.

And then she hit on a different strategy. When I turned ten she asked me if I'd like to celebrate my birthday at a fancy French restaurant. "I know a good place," she said. "It's very elegant and expensive. We'll get all dressed up and it will be a big splurge."

My mother looked at me with such excitement that I conceived the ambition, then and there, of becoming an especially elegant ten-year-old, of the sort to inspire love in distracted parents. I would become a gourmet.

But doing so turned out to be far more complicated than I expected. At home, getting ready to leave for the restaurant, my father threw a blue blazer over a plaid shirt and old chinos and then stood in the middle of the living room, showing off his bare ankles and beat-up boat shoes. "What do you think?" he asked my mother, looking pleased with himself.

My mother, in a silk dress and heavy jewelry, checked her watch. "What exactly are you trying to prove?"

"Nothing, except that I make enough money I don't have to care what other people think. Their petty judgments and cheap snobberies mean nothing to me. Nothing!"

"I'm more interested in why you want to ruin the child's birthday."

"That's not the point! The point is comfort!"

Even after my father put on socks, the evening felt like a fragile enterprise, teetering on the edge of sorrow and humiliation. The restaurant was an old chestnut called the Forum of the Twelve Caesars, and it was lined with marble columns on which sat the busts of noble Romans, watching the patrons feed. It looked incredibly grand to me, and the very fact of our presence there, at a little table toward the back, seemed to imply some hope that we weren't merely gluttonous and self-absorbed, and that I wasn't in danger of weeping. We were a family of elegant gastronomes who ate among Caesars. We would prosper and be loved.

"Wasn't that fun?" my mother said later that night, back at home. "We should make a tradition of it, don't you think?"

"Yes," I said, confused. Fun didn't seem to be the point, exactly: the point was something beyond my understanding. The best I could make out, very dimly, was that our family was in some kind of deep and subtle trouble and our only hope was to eat complicated, delicate foods amid the hushed clink of heavy silverware. That my father didn't understand this, that he resisted it, made it all the more urgent.

Every year after that, on my birthday, we went to another dizzyingly expensive restaurant picked by my mother; my father tried to wear (or not wear) something that would disrupt the occasion; and I attempted to make elegant dinner conversation while vibrating with nearly religious levels of hope, self-consciousness, and disappointment. We ate duck with figs at the Four Seasons, caviar and blinis at the Russian Tea Room. And then the year I was to turn fourteen, my mother said, "I was thinking it might be fun to do this one in France."

"France?"

She explained that her friend Eleanor was going with a friend from work in the summer; we could join up with them for a three-week trip across the country, going from restaurant to restaurant, sightseeing during the day and eating at night.

"What about everyone else?" I asked, meaning the rest of the family.

"Your father hates to travel, and David and Perrin are too little for this kind of trip."

Even better, I thought. Elegant restaurants in France without my brother and sister, who were always crowding my act and stealing applause, without my father, who made our attempts at fine dining look ridiculous and doomed. My mother and I would go and join the tribe of sophisticated, happy gourmets without them.

IN 1976 PARIS HAD no air-conditioning and was thus unequipped for the worst heat wave in one hundred years. We spent our nights staring at the ceiling, unable to sleep, and our days drifting through the Louvre in a dreamlike confusion. Out on the street, the city was like a gorgeous cake baking in some kind of weird blue oven—hotter and hotter, about to burn. We sat listlessly in cafés, drinking Cokes, too tired to get up.

But as the dinner hour approached, a change would come over us: back at the hotel, my mother would open her huge suitcase and get herself into one of her many heavily beaded outfits; I would put on the only pair of dressy pants I'd remembered to pack, which happened to be thick wool; and we would go down to the lobby to meet Eleanor and her friend Mary, two large, pale figures in polyester slacks, burdened with enormous tote bags and gigantic purses. The four of us would then head off to the next Michelin-starred restaurant on our list.

For once our food obsession really managed to transport us beyond rancor. Seated at a table in a velvet-walled dining room in which not a breeze stirred, we would eat four or five courses with insane gusto, the discontented and panicked parts of us appeased and quieted. Stumbling out into the steamy Parisian evening, we were at peace.

Our last night before leaving the city for the countryside, it was so hot that I stripped to my underwear, wrapped myself in wet towels, and lay on my bed in the dark, trying to cool down enough to sleep. My mother spoke from her bed across the room.

"Those snails," she said.

"That seafood thing," I said.

That evening we had eaten in a nouvelle seafood place that seemed to be inspired by Japanese cuisine: things were raw or lightly cooked, absolutely fresh, served with varieties of seaweeds. My dish was a sort of bouillabaisse without broth, a collection of shellfish and other sea creatures piled in a big bowl like a floral arrangement.

"I think you're starting to understand the true beauty of food," she said.

"I think I am," I answered, rearranging my towels.

"Your father will never understand."

That was because he basically treated food like an alcoholic treats whiskey, as a form of solace and forgetting. A fight with my mother would send him wandering across the city all night, eating inhuman amounts of falafel and shawarma, cheesecake and cannoli. We would find him passed out on the couch in the morning, surrounded by empty takeout containers.

While my mother thought that fine dining would save us from the suspicion that we were worthless, my father believed that eating would protect us from sorrow—that we just needed to do more and more of it, a physical deluge, an orgy of gnawing and chomping.

"He eats because he's sad," I said to her.

"Yes, but it's so much better to eat because you're happy."

I'd come to France because I wanted my mother's attention free of competition from my siblings and my father, but sharing a room with her felt a little odd—a little too much. She was in a nightgown, I was in my underwear and some wet towels, and I remember having to ignore the weirdness of the situation, the suspicion that I was actually too old for such unbounded intimacy, even if I still wanted it.

For her part, she seemed delighted to have a roommate, someone to talk to. She was always incurably lonely, the kind of person who would talk till dawn, night after night, if you were willing to listen. She wanted to explain herself.

"I went to Paris for the first time right after finishing law school," she said to me. "And the first thing I did was sit down in a café and eat a little bowl of wild strawberries in cream. They tasted like perfume, and I knew then that I would never live in Brooklyn again. Your father doesn't understand that."

"But we don't live in Brooklyn."

"That's because of me. If it were up to him, we'd still be living next to his relatives on Brown Street."

The truth was that I liked my father's relatives, liked the rolled cabbage and *cholent* they served, the way they all sat on their porches and talked across the low brick walls to each other. My own family seemed isolated and sad in comparison. "They always look so happy," I said.

"Because they're so limited." *Limited* was the worst thing my mother could say about somebody, implying ignorance, blindness, stupidity, lack of sophistication, and a resistance to the enlarging powers of culture. "They don't know there's a world beyond Sheepshead Bay."

"Sheepshead Bay is part of the world, too."

"Yes, but it's a very boring part."

My mother talked often about the frustration of living among people who collected porcelain figurines of shepherds and shepherdesses and sheathed their furniture in clear plastic to keep it clean, who had never been to the Museum of Modern Art, even though it was just a subway ride away, and didn't see why she had to go, either. My response was usually a studied blandness, the only method I knew to avoid the fact that she was talking about our relatives and, by extension, my father.

"Well, nothing beats Paris," I said blandly.

"Yes, the city of art and cathedrals," she said, "and strawberries in crème fraîche."

THE NEXT MORNING, WE got our rental car and left the city. Eleanor drove; my mother and I sat in back, Mary in the passenger seat up front. We were on our way to a series of great restaurants, including Troisgros in Roanne, Bocuse in Lyon, La Pyramide in Vienne. The mood in the car was ebullient, hungry.

"Somewhere out there is the perfect meal," said my mother.

Eleanor laughed. "And we are going to find it."

Like my mother, Eleanor had emerged from her childhood in Brooklyn ravenous for culture. But otherwise the two women were inside-out versions of each other. My mother wanted to dress up in something splendid and prove herself worthy of joining the secret society of the urbane and the beautiful. Eleanor didn't need to dress up because she had no illusion of ever being allowed to join anything: she weighed two hundred pounds, worked at the welfare department, and still lived in Flatbush with her mother, Bobby, in a house I remember as perpetually dark because they kept the lights off to save money. She reused wax paper and tinfoil, saved rubber bands, took her lunch to work in a paper bag, and kept a little notebook in her purse in which she wrote down everything she spent as soon as she spent it. She did all this so she could afford three weeks in France in the summer, eating in the best restaurants in the world.

Conflict was inevitable, I guess, but the form it took was odd. Eleanor had made all the reservations and plotted the route, and had done so with near-military precision, budgeting just enough time to leave the château or castle we were touring, park the car, and run into the restaurant before we would lose our table. In Paris my mother and I had been on our own most of the day; we'd always been able to go back to the hotel and dress for dinner. But now we couldn't even wash the day's sweat from our faces because we were trapped in the back seat of the rental car as we raced to make our reservation.

At La Pyramide we walked across the parking lot to a restaurant that looked like a magical fairy castle lit up in the gloaming. We were grimy, dressed in shorts. As we made our way to our table in the garden, I could see my mother examining the other diners, carefully assessing the Frenchwomen in their silks and jewelry. These people would never know that she had a load of beautiful clothes in her suitcase, that she was a lawyer by training, one of only two women in her class at Brooklyn Law. They would think she was a tourist from Sheepshead Bay.

"I don't care about the money," she said in our hotel room later, after an argument with Eleanor over who had ordered the second bottle of mineral water, "but I don't like to be cheated."

"She's not cheating you."

"I think she is." She was standing at her open suitcase, running her hands through her neatly folded dinner outfits, the silks and satins. What she meant was that she had been cheated out of the chance to be beautiful and admired, but she couldn't say it so directly. "I can't let her ruin your birthday trip," she said.

It took me a moment to remember that all of this was supposedly for my birthday. Suddenly I was full of the same incoherent mixture of yearning and disappointment that I'd experienced at the Forum of the Twelve Caesars, sitting under the gaze of Roman senators as my parents bickered. Instead of being elegant and refined, we were boorish and petty, doomed to frustration and bafflement.

I could never win an argument with my mother, but my response had a certain primitive integrity to it: I went to bed and fell violently ill during the night, and the next morning I rode in the car, feverish and shivering, wrapped in a blanket stolen from the hotel we'd just left.

In the afternoon, I slept in the back seat of the parked car as the three women explored a medieval town and a famous cathedral. That night, I wore a sweater into the stiflingly hot restaurant. I still managed to gobble down four courses, the flavors intensified, made almost visual, by the fever: pork rillettes that tasted of the forest shade, thinly sliced duck breast with fresh apricots . . . By the end, I was light, floating, certain that all would be well if I could only sleep for a long, long time.

Then, through some kind of karmic algorithm, Eleanor fell sick. It started with a thin, accordion-like wheeze and soon became a terrible hacking cough. In the days that followed she drove many hundreds of kilometers of winding country roads, forced herself up the stone steps of every ancient castle and medieval hill town on the itinerary, then ate a gigantic dinner late into the night, in spite of being ferociously ill. It sounds almost comical now—tourism as a sort of insane endurance sport—but it was awful to watch. In churches and museums, she leaned against the walls as if she was going to slip to her knees. During dinner she dozed between courses, snoring.

It's only now, older than she was then, that I understand. She'd spent the entire year saving for that trip, skimping so she could splurge on foie gras and truffles for three weeks in France—so she could be cultured, a gourmet. She didn't have to enjoy it, but she had to *have* it. If not, she was left with nothing but the house in Brooklyn she shared with Bobby, her desk at the welfare department, and her hunger for something more.

One afternoon, full of decongestants, she fell asleep at the wheel. We careened into a guardrail at full speed and ricocheted back into traffic; all these years later I can still summon up the feeling of sliding sideways, the sound of my mother's high scream trailing above us. Awake, Eleanor swerved left and then right, struggling to regain control of the car, and maybe the oddest thing about that incredible, dreamlike interlude was that we were all unhurt at the end of it—even the car got by with just a single long scrape down the side.

That night in our hotel room, a little giddy, my mother and I ran over the details of the accident, leaching out the strangeness and the fear. "That scream of yours," I said. "My ears are still ringing."

"I was trying to wake her up."

"I think the guardrail did that."

The one thing we didn't want to talk about was the next morning. If we didn't go with Eleanor, we would have to figure out how to get back to Paris by ourselves, and as people of refined sensibilities we could not be bothered with bus tickets and train schedules, which is to say that we were secretly afraid of getting lost and looking like fools. So we made jokes till we fell asleep, and the next day climbed into the slightly scarred rental car as if nothing had happened.

I'm still struck, so many years later, by the blithe denial involved in that choice. Then again, what was Eleanor but a stand-in for my father, the philistine we depended on for our cultural pursuits? At home, my father did all the driving, while my mother, who had never learned to drive, sat in the passenger seat, reading a book, and I sat in back. He would drive us to a museum or to a theater and then sleep in the parked car until it was time to drive us back home. Being chauffeured had become such a fundamental part of our relationship to the world that we couldn't imagine an alternative—even as we huddled in our seats in the little rental car, gasping with fear at each bump in the road.

Weirdly, the days that followed the accident were the best of the trip: we were just so glad to be among the living. Buttering a piece of bread now felt like a form of prayer, and cutting meat from the bone a benediction. In the little town of Mougins, at a restaurant called Moulin de Mougins ("Picasso's favorite," my mother told me), I had fish quenelles that left me in a state of wordless gratitude. It wasn't that we were finally elegant, because we weren't and probably never would be. But each mouthful of fish made me happier to be who I actually was, and when I stepped out of the restaurant the beauty of our surroundings was almost heartbreaking: the delicate white light, the flash of red bougainvillea overflowing a whitewashed wall. I remember being so full of joy that I simply began running down the road as fast as I could, starving for the whole world and all the gorgeous things in it.

My father and siblings met us at the airport. During the car ride home, my mother talked in a giddy rush, as she did whenever she was nervous or uncertain. Maybe she had mixed feelings about being back, or was disappointed by the trip itself. Maybe that's why she expounded in such relentless detail how excellent it was, what a huge educational experience, how I'd become an international traveler, a lover of beauty, a discerning gourmet. Maybe that's why she left out all the bad parts, including the crash. While she talked I nodded, listening carefully so I'd know what to think about the confusing mess of events that had happened to us.

My father must have had his own complicated feelings after three weeks spent parenting two children alone, but he responded as he did to any emotional situation: "You must be hungry," he said.

It was in fact dinnertime by the look of the light outside the car window, the row houses by the highway turning golden as we sped by. Instead of going home he drove us to a restaurant in Chinatown, where we ate till we could hardly move, the plates piling up, black bean sauce sloshing on the table. Butterfish, razor clams, salted squid, crabs in ginger—the dishes kept on coming.

"More?" asked my father.

"More," I said, knowing instinctively that this was the right answer to the question we were circling. Across the table, my mother assiduously twisted snails from their shells with a long thin fork, then threw the shells in a bowl. We ate in order to wipe away the confusion of whatever mission we had just returned from, to knit ourselves back together, to be a family again. And then we paused, out of breath, stunned.

My father leaned back in his seat, giving space to his huge belly. "Does anyone have a stretcher? I think I just injured myself."

We talked woozily about plans for the weekend, as if trying to wake up and figure out where we were. We could have lunch at the Second Avenue Deli and dinner at Victor's Cuban. Or we could try that new Ethiopian place, where you got to eat with your hands.

"What about a French restaurant?" asked my mother, ever hopeful. "Robert and I will show you what to order."

But I didn't want to show anyone what to order; it was too hard, too confusing. "Air," I said, pushing myself up from the table.

Outside, the street was hot and sticky. The light was a dark blue, and the atmosphere was luminous, full of people and cars and big signs in Chinese: the exact opposite of Mougins, but just as beautiful. I stood for a while, taking it all in, feeling the sense of possibility, and then I turned and looked through the restaurant window. There was our table, and there was my family. My mother was feeding my father a chunk of pine-apple, and he was laughing.

Two Angels

She was my father's secretary and very lovely in ways I couldn't quite describe—at nine years old, my mind didn't yet include the idea of female beauty. School was on break, and maybe because my parents didn't know what to do with me, she and I had been at her desk behind the reception window the last couple of days in an intense interaction that felt like the deepest intimacy.

"I'm going to show you something," she said, reaching into her pocketbook and bringing out a rectangular jeweler's box, then flipping open the lid: inside was a shiny military decoration with a big black swastika in the middle. She ran a finger over the swastika's black enamel surface. "It's real. My boyfriend gave it to me."

I glanced up at her, confused. I had never considered the possibility that she had a boyfriend—that she had any life beyond the desk, our two chairs. The idea was as strange as the medal, the sinister elbows of the swastika.

"My boyfriend is a Hells Angel," she explained. "The SS were the elite of the German army, the bravest of the brave, just like the Hells Angels."

I listened in silence, worried that she knew we were Jewish, until at some point she put the medal back in her purse. Then I began telling her a story of my own, using a small rubber kangaroo I had brought with me.

I've forgotten the details, but I remember feeling a little ashamed of myself because the story came off younger than I wanted to sound. And yet I couldn't stop myself. I was in a rush, bent on regaining our connection, the feeling that there was nobody in the world but the two of us.

And then a man stepped through the front door. In my memory he is gigantic, his head almost grazing the ceiling. He stopped at the reception window and thrust his face through the opening: black eyes, black beard, long black hair. I froze with the rubber kangaroo in my hand, and she looked up at him with an expression both annoyed and embarrassed. "This is what we do all day," she told him.

He glanced my way. "Hey, are you bothering my girlfriend?" he boomed. Then my father came out and greeted him and together they walked back to his office.

That was the final rupture. After that, instead of sitting with her, I roamed the office suite, listening in on my father's conversations with his clients, or poking around the magazine rack in the waiting area. Finally, I drifted into the conference room, where I found a stack of *Playboys* in a cardboard box and sat on the carpet and leafed through them with a hovering, silent feeling. I had never seen pictures of naked women before.

I sensed a presence behind me and turned my head to see another one of the Angels standing in the doorway. Big Vinnie Girolama was so large that he completely filled the opening: no shirt, just a leather vest with the Hells Angels insignia on it, his big belly covered in tattoos. The expression on his face was oddly thoughtful, and he left in silence; I went back to turning pages.

Some time later, I watched my father walking with him down the hall to the reception area, seeing him off, and I heard Vinnie say, "I'm just telling you this, Stan, because I know if it were my son, I'd want somebody to tell me. That's all."

"Of course, of course," said my father, who was in fact incredibly prim in this one area of life. "It's okay, I like *Playboy* too."

EVERYONE WANTS TO BE A HELLS ANGEL

THE CREDITS FOR THE biker documentary *Hells Angels Forever* list five directors, six producers, three writers, four editors, and a crew of over sixty, which is to say that the production was long and a lot of people dropped out or were forced out. The project originated with Leon Gast, a documentarian who would go on to win an Academy Award for *When We Were Kings*, about the Muhammad Ali–George Foreman fight in Zaire. Gast was replaced on *Hells Angels* by Sandy Alexander, the president of the club's New York chapter, who had never made a film before.

"They were talking off in a corner," my father told me, right after it happened—I must have been eleven or twelve years old. "And then Sandy slapped him so hard it sounded like a gunshot. Leon fell down, and then he jumped up and started to run. Nobody's seen him since."

My father represented the club, but he was also a gentle man who rarely raised his voice, and he looked genuinely abashed by what he had seen. It wasn't till I started to laugh that he began laughing, too, a little sheepishly. The rule in our house was that the Angels were *characters*; whatever they did had to be discussed with an air of wry amusement.

"The contract gave him complete creative control," my father told me, "but I thought he *understood*." Understood that things had to be done the Angels' way. "I mean, who could be that stupid?"

"What's going to happen to the movie?" I asked.

It turned out that Gast had left his equipment behind and the Angels were using it to carry on. "The inmates are running the asylum," my father said, starting to look genuinely amused now, the unpleasantness of the slap forgotten. "Whatever happens will at least be interesting."

A few years later, my parents went to a showing of an early cut of the film. I remember them getting dressed up to go out, remember that my siblings and I were left behind at home, resentful. The next morning, they described the movie to us, and I felt as if I'd missed the most important event in the world. "Your father has a scene with Herman Graber," said my mother. Herman Graber, my father's law partner, was always called by his full name to signal that he was a comic character, too, straight man for my father's jokes. "Your father keeps cutting him off so he can hog the camera for himself." We all laughed. Dad was a star.

I tried to get him to take me to one of the big block parties outside the clubhouse on East Third Street, but he wouldn't consider it. "The Angels are absolute pussycats, except when they're high. When they're high you have to know how to handle them."

"How?"

"I tell a joke."

Instead, he took me to the clubhouse on weekend afternoons, and we stood around on the sidewalk, talking motorcycles and law with the Angels outside. Big Vinnie Girolama was usually there, his body so immense that his head looked small. There was a silver ring in his nose and a black pirate's beard down his chest, and he was usually shirtless, his big stomach covered in gothic script, KILL OR BE KILLED, on the inside of his forearm. I stood as close to my father as possible, silent, watchful. These were the characters in our story, but in person they weren't *comic*. They were something else I couldn't quite allow myself to register.

My father would tell me to wait in the car and then he and Sandy Alexander would walk into the tenement entrance that led upstairs, past the signs saying KEEP OUT and ANYONE CAUGHT STEALING LIGHT BULBS WILL HAVE THEIR ARM BROKEN. I would go back to the car and sit for what felt like a very long time, feeling the minutes accumulate, wondering when he'd get back, then wondering if he'd ever come back, if he was gone forever. My whole body electric.

Is it okay to use the term *separation anxiety* at the age of seven, eight, nine? I want to put it closer to the way I experienced it: I knew deep in my bones that my father loved me, but if you told me he was never coming back, I would have believed you.

The only time I was allowed to follow them upstairs, I found myself in a room that was ordinary except for one magical detail: a big bird cage with a baby monkey sitting inside, looking highly aggrieved. While my father and Sandy conferred in low voices off by the window, I stuck my finger through the bars of the cage, until the monkey finally leaped forward and bit me. The pain of his razor-like teeth was sharp, stinging. Examining the tiny wound with its trace of blood, I became instantly certain that I'd contracted rabies: I could picture the disease traveling through my bloodstream like tiny bubbles. For weeks, I watched for signs of insanity. But I didn't say a word to anyone.

A couple of years later—I must have been eleven—I went with my father to a rock concert on a ferry boat sailing up the Hudson, the climax of *Hells Angels Forever.* Two Angels lifted us aboard from the little launch that got us there, and then my father disappeared and I spent the rest of the night walking anxious circles around the ship, searching for him. My sense of panic mixed with the strange beauty of the event, the pink sunset and the darkness, the oily black shimmer of the river and the slow-moving lights of Manhattan. Men and women stood around listening to the music, wrapped in their indecipherable grown-up world. Angels danced what looked like war dances, fists in the air. I moved through it all, invisible.

When I finally found him, he explained that he had taken shelter in the pilothouse with the captain and crew against the crazed bacchanal outside. "We barricaded the door! No way we were going out in that insanity!"

There was nothing I could say after that. This was an Angels story, I realized, and the rule was that you had to laugh.

"Time to go home," he said, taking my hand.

Jump ahead forty years. My father had been dead for a decade, and I'd forgotten all about *Hells Angels Forever.* I was living with my wife and children in Taiwan for the year, in an old Japanese colonial house that was succumbing to tropical rot: geckos scrambling over the ceilings, chasing each other; great rolling thunderstorms that would send ants climbing the walls in organized columns, like armies. I had terrible insomnia and would wander the house all night, so happy to be on this adventure and so deeply sad at the same time, for reasons I didn't quite understand. It was as if the happiness was making me sadder and more frightened, lonelier, threatening to pull me in two. Standing in the dark of the living room on that particular night, listening to the clicking sound of the lizards on the ceiling, I suddenly missed my father so much that I opened my laptop and typed his name into the search bar. There was *Hells Angels Forever* on YouTube, and at twenty-nine minutes in, there was my father.

He is seated with Herman Graber at a conference table in their office: soft, heavy men in wide ties and long sideburns. Herman explains to the camera not to be fooled by the swastikas and Nazi regalia, that the Angels are patriots, enthusiastic supporters of the Vietnam War, what you might in fact call right-wingers. He pauses, blinks, concerned that he might have gone too far. "But not Fascists, no, nothing like that."

My father cuts in. "Perhaps best suited to the most conservative wing of the Republican party—the Goldwater wing."

Herman nods cautiously. My father suppresses a smile. He is forty-four, his face handsome but heavy, with big brown eyes that drift off into private thought, then return to the camera, mischievous. His expression is sweet and slightly wounded, as if he is worried that you won't like him, that he's said something to offend you. And then his hand straightens his tie, a gesture so familiar to me that I can almost feel that hand resting on my shoulder, very lightly, as it used to. My whole body grows warm with his presence.

At dawn, I got up and went to the window: egrets, shaggy and white, were in the pond behind the house. When the rest of the family woke up, I took them to our local Taoist temple to make an offering. It was something we hadn't done before, though I knew how it worked: food for the deities and then ritual money for the ancestor, to be burnt in the brick stove.

"Why are we doing this?" asked my son, Jonah. I could see that he was afraid we would embarrass ourselves at the temple.

I did not tell him about the movie. "Your grandfather's been dead ten years. He probably needs a little cash."

My father once came home with a brown paper bag full of money. He dumped it out on the dining room table and then reached over and started counting the bills out into neat little stacks. When he was done he asked my mother to help him double-check his figures, and they started counting their way down the length of the table together. My parents were so often at odds that it looked like something deep and very beautiful was happening.

My father and I went to Saks Fifth Avenue the next day, all mirrors and marble columns. He hardly glanced as he pulled things down from the shelves, a salesman walking behind us to carry the clothes. Back then, I assumed that was how everyone dealt with money: burned through it in one single ecstatic cataclysm that left nothing behind. A few days later, I caught him writing on the outside of an envelope containing a bill: DECEASED RETURN TO SENDER.

At the Taoist temple, the other worshippers showed us how to make our offerings. We placed a plastic container of sliced pineapple on the table beside the shrine, lit incense sticks, and bowed to the deity, a delighted old man with a white beard and tall forehead. Then we bought stacks of ritual money, a sort of play money that looked better than the real thing: pink, red, yellow, and green paper, stamped with gold leaf and red ink. We took the bills over to the stove and counted them off in bunches, throwing them in and watching them blacken and curl.

I had been too resentful to say Kaddish for him after his death. It felt to me as if he were pulling one of his old disappearing acts, in which he left me waiting in the car and climbed the stairs into the Hells Angels clubhouse. But now I was trying to make it up to him, throwing bills into the stove as fast as I could. The heat from the opening was like a shove in the face, pushing me back. I held up a wad of pink and gold money; the wind from the fire snatched it from my hand, hungry.

THE ANGELS GAVE HIM his first motorcycle as a thank-you gift: not a big chopped hog but a dainty little orange Yamaha, befitting his civilian status. It was just the thing for him: he was extremely heavy, and it made him feel light and fast. In traffic, he'd shoot through the narrow gap between stopped cars, onto the sidewalk if he was in a real rush. He could get me to school in a few zigs and zags. He could park anywhere. His picture was in the *Post* with a little squib attached, something like "Hells Angel Lawyer Rides Around Town on Motorcycle." But he was already studying motorcycle magazines, figuring out his next step. Soon he'd traded up to a gigantic German machine with a humped tank, the engine a slab of silver muscle. When he got on, his toes just barely touched the ground. We'd go for long rides upstate, faster and faster till the scenery blurred and my fingers hurt from gripping the little rail that ran around the back of the seat.

"It's the best therapy there is," my father told me.

We went on a cross-country motorcycle trip when I was sixteen, from New York to Los Angeles and back. I rode behind him, feet up on pegs above the mufflers, hands gripping a flimsy rail that looped around the rear of my seat. Long days of straight roads at tremendous speeds, the scenery an unreal streak, but through some visual quirk the pavement beneath my feet granularly precise, as if it were barely moving. At night, in a motel, my father in the other bed, snoring, I felt as if I were still flying through the darkness.

Before reaching L.A., we stopped in Las Vegas and stayed in a big fancy hotel attached to a casino. I wandered behind my father, who watched the players pulling the levers of slot machines. "Some of these people will go home wearing nothing but a barrel," he said.

"Let's try our luck," I said to him.

"You always lose." He walked on, and it became clear that he had no intention of sitting down at one of the machines. "Your grandfather had a gambling problem. Nana had to mortgage the house once."

My grandfather had died when I was a baby and I had no memory of him, but I thought of my grandmother's house in Sheepshead Bay, Brooklyn, the tiny rooms and the little back porch with the clothesline. I don't believe I'd ever seen her outside of that house. "So why are we here?" I asked.

"The buffet."

In that restaurant, we moved down the length of the steam table, piling our plates. It was all-you-can-eat, so the more we consumed, the more it approached free, and that became the goal: we wanted to do damage, to get back some of what had been lost to the slot machines by the millions of gamblers who passed through town. My father ate even as we stood in line, and then he continued in silence at our table, unreachable, his personality shrunk back behind his eyes. Champagne glasses of chocolate mousse lined up in front of him like an assembly line: two swipes of his spoon, push the glass to the side, and on to the next. I tried to keep up, feeling myself filling like a helium balloon, beginning to rise in some dreamy, abstract way. I sank down in my seat. My eyes fluttered.

We spent a number of days repeating this pattern, wandering the casino and watching the foolishness, eating sickening amounts of food at virtually no cost, lying in our beds watching movies in the room, doing the dead man's float in the indoor pool, facedown.

When we left Las Vegas, it was a relief to be moving again. And then one time, on a stretch of long straight highway, I looked over and saw him holding his hands up in the air, hovering a little above the handlebars as if he were performing a magic trick. I held my breath, trying to stay absolutely still. I could feel the delicate balance as we hurtled down the road like a missile, could feel it in my stomach.

At a gas station, I said to him, "Could you do me a favor and keep your hands on the handlebars next time?"

His face looked surprised, as if he were only now remembering what he'd done, and then I could see him thinking, putting the pieces together. "You don't think I'd put you in any danger, do you?"

"No." The idea was impossible. It's not what I'd meant at all; I trusted him completely.

"Of course not," he said, touching his hand to my cheek. "I would never put you in any danger. You know that."

I did know that, but he kept on doing it, and we kept arguing about it afterward. "You did it again," I'd say.

"I'm sorry, I forgot." He looked crestfallen.

"You promised you wouldn't."

"My hands get tired."

"Then we'll stop and rest."

"Now that I understand how much it bothers you, I won't do it."

But of course he did. Each time, I felt as if I were flying through the air, saw from way back inside my head how precarious, almost accidental, it was to be alive. I wanted to beat my fists on his back and scream that I hated him, that he was a menace, a liar, but I also knew that I had to stay absolutely still, that I had to use every bit of myself to transmit calm thoughts: hold on to the handlebars, the handlebars, hold on. Then, when it was over and the ride was done, and we were standing on the pavement in front of a motel or a restaurant, legs still vibrating from hours on the bike, I would feel a wave of guilt come over me. Because he had already forgotten.

YEARS BEFORE THAT, I remember going with my father to Junior's Delicatessen one night, sitting at the counter and ordering cheesecake. We had eaten dinner somewhere else and were there just for dessert—though we'd already had dessert at that other place, too. In this kind of mood he was silent, preoccupied. The office was not doing well: a client had left him; another owed him money and wasn't paying. While we waited, he took the tongs from one of the silver urns full of pickles, put a few on a little plate, and ate them in what must have been a single second. I remember there was a little green tomato—I didn't like tomatoes. After that, he just reached into the urn with his hand. It was like some kind of line had been crossed. Head down, he ate mechanically, reaching in, pulling out a pickle and putting it in his mouth, reaching in again and pulling out another.

I had grown up with scenes like this, but they always made me panicky. I watched with a kind of frightened intensity.

"Hey, look at him," the guy a couple of empty seats down from us said to the counterman, who had his back turned. "He's eating the pickles with his fingers."

It didn't really help that by the time the counterman turned around, my father had finished every last pickle in the urn and was sitting quite still, a little stunned. That outraged the man even more. "I'm not eating from there," he said, pointing to the urn.

"He's not doing anything," said the counterman.

"But he was."

"Look at him, he's not."

My father watched them argue as if it had nothing at all to do with him, his eyes clouded.

That began a familiar cycle. His weight ballooned up from handsome to heavy, and then to very heavy, and then past that to the sort of extreme obesity where people see nothing but a fat man. The fancy clothes didn't fit; he found old ones, and then they didn't fit, either. He couldn't button his shirt or his pants. He stopped wearing socks, tying his shoes, combing his hair, shaving, showering. The world began to treat us differently. When we walked into a candy store, the cash register guy's eyes narrowed, trying to assess what form of trouble we were, whether we meant to shoplift. We got variations on that look wherever we went, on a continuum from mockery to dismissal. When we walked into an expensive steak house (because, weirdly, we changed none of our habits, as if nothing were happening to us and we looked the same), the face of the maître d' flickered, and I knew we were in for a very long wait, with all the beautifully suited businessmen going in ahead of us.

I hated the well dressed.

There was the night he put on an enormous green windbreaker to take me to the opera. He knew most of Puccini by heart and had season tickets in the dead center of the orchestra—by which I mean we deserved to be there as much as anyone else. But he could barely get himself together to go.

"Can't you wear something else?" my mother said to him, as he and I were getting ready to leave.

"Why?" he asked.

"It's the opera. And that's a windbreaker."

"I need it because of my shirt," he growled, and he pulled the windbreaker open in a kind of Superman gesture. Underneath was an old blue work shirt, open to his belly button because it was missing so many buttons.

"So change it," she said.

"I don't have anything else." He zipped the windbreaker back up to his chin and we left for the Met. The car ride was silent. At a red light, he closed his eyes and actually dozed for a second. He wasn't getting much sleep at night, watching TV till dawn.

"Light's green," I told him. His eyes opened, he stomped on the gas, and we shot forward. My anxiety seemed to have something to do with the dark and the streetlights, nothing at all to do with the shirt or the windbreaker, and once we were in our red-velvet seats I started to feel hopeful. The layer-cake theater, the chandeliers like frozen explosions in the space above our heads: this was the world I wanted to live in. Maybe the windbreaker would stay zipped and nobody would know; maybe we would be allowed to stay. But when the music started, my father began nodding off. I gave him a poke; he startled awake, but then he began to snore and I couldn't wake him. An old man behind us, white haired and irate, reached forward and clopped him on the shoulder. "Stop that!" he hissed. "Where do you think you are?"

My father sat upright, eyes big. He didn't turn around, simply stared straight ahead. I did the same, my heart pumping hard. The stage seemed a million miles away, the music just a form of noise.

The next afternoon, we stood outside the Hells Angels clubhouse, feeling bruised. My father's eyes were red from lack of sleep. He was wearing the same windbreaker, but now it was open and I could see the shirt underneath, the same shirt with the missing buttons and the big stains. None of that mattered here. We felt safe among the choppers and the gigantic men in oily jeans and tattoos. In this atmosphere, we could be the normal ones, the representatives of middle-class decency. The operagoers in their finery were something else, what in the movie is called "Nixon's America," prejudiced and stupid.

We never talked about what happened at the opera. We talked a lot about anti-Semitism, incredibly, as if that explained why people stared at us when we walked into a store, why we had to wait so long for a table at Peter Luger. We talked about police overreach and the erosion of civil rights. We talked about the Angels, too, the incredible roar of their choppers, the scariness of their outfits. The Angels demanded respect; nobody messed with them. We were too eager to be liked; our feelings were fragile; we ached with our own vulnerability. It was a form of weakness we wanted to rid ourselves of, but we didn't know how.

A couple of years later, we came home to our apartment and found all the stereo equipment gone. My father called a fence he knew and learned that a group of teenagers had done it; they lived in a public housing project just a short walk away. Then he called Sandy Alexander. Sandy, Vinnie, and a couple of other Angels came to the house. The plan was for them to accompany my father to the building where the kids lived. My father had already spoken to one of the parents; a time had been set up to meet and talk. That's when I inserted myself into the proceedings. I wanted to be included. My stereo had been taken, too, I said. We couldn't let ourselves be pushed around anymore. I had some vague idea of watching the kids grovel in fear. My father looked at me, annoyed, but said okay, I could come.

It felt all wrong from the start. The Angels were in their gear, wearing the vests with the death's-head insignia, but they looked bored and impatient, as if this were a task and not revenge. They weren't angry. They weren't even scary, really. They were *reasonable*. It was so disappointing. Together, we went down to the street and walked to where the kids lived, in some project-y buildings a couple of blocks up Second Avenue. On the way, we passed the supermarket, the dry cleaners, the optometrist, the pet store, ordinary shops that seemed to exist in a haze of low-level boredom. We were in the wrong movie.

"We need to keep this low-key," said Sandy, as we waited in the lobby for the elevator. The building was fairly new but already falling apart. Public housing. Bare of decoration. Dirty. I had never been any place that looked quite like it.

"Exactly," said my father, clearly relieved that there was agreement. "They're just a bunch of kids. They've got adults egging them on to do this."

"Get the stuff back, that's all," said Big Vinnie. "No mess, no problems."

The elevator was so rickety, I didn't think we'd make it. It was a high floor, a long dirty hallway. A woman came to the door and let us in, a heavyset Hispanic woman who looked as if she had seen many trials. She took one disapproving glance at me and marched me into a back bedroom where a bunch of kids sat waiting tensely: the thieves. We nodded to each other, and I sat down in the circle. The room was a wreck; I remember glancing through the door and seeing the Angels seated at the dining room table talking like an interview committee to the woman. "They're just kids," said Sandy, "but there are adults who put them up to bad things."

"Right," said Vinnie, "they're misguided. We know it's not their fault."

The woman listened stonily because she had no choice. The kids had trashed the room in which I sat, clearly: there was graffiti on the wall, a hole punched in the plasterboard. Why did their mother allow that? I was used to lots of nice things and there was nothing nice, just a pile of mattresses. The kids themselves sat around, silent, smirking, cowed.

Back out on the street, the Angels left us and walked uptown. My father and I walked home in silence together. The kids came later that day, carrying our things. But they were just things now. I didn't want them anymore.

I WAS IN MY mid-teens when I first saw *Hells Angels Forever.* I remember the incredible excitement. My father appeared only twice, for all of three or four minutes, but to me he seemed to be everywhere in it, as if the movie were really about him and not the Angels, or the Angels were really about him in some magical way. There's Sandy! There's Vinnie! There's a bunch of Angels shooting at bottles in a river! There's the clubhouse. There were faces I couldn't name, names I couldn't place with faces. I'd heard stories about all of them, told in my father's perpetually amused voice while sitting in one or another delicatessen at ten at night, eating a pastrami sandwich, feeling safe from the world, feeling useful and loved.

In an interview on-screen, an Angel says, "There ain't a man alive who at one time or another hasn't wanted to be a Hells Angel. I don't care whether he's a lawyer, judge, preacher, or what."

Nowadays, I watch with more complicated emotions. The Angel who speaks those words is wearing a T-shirt that says WHITE POWER. Later, in a scene from the boat concert, an African American performer by the name of Bo Diddley sings a song called "Do Your Thing": *You got to do your thing, you got to do your thing. If it feels good, do it.* I think about how he might have felt playing for a group of bikers in swastikas and white-power T-shirts, how he might have rationalized that decision. Then I think about how *we* rationalized our decisions, and I am equally perplexed. I was wandering the ship's deck while Bo Diddley sang that song, looking for my father. Was he really in the pilothouse? Why didn't he take me with him?

Meanwhile, "Do Your Thing" continues to play over a montage of Angels beating people up. The footage is from different places and times, but the violence always involves one guy wailing on somebody who offers no resistance, just waiting it out. Then the aggressor drifts off and another Angel starts punching.

Earlier in the film, Big Vinnie has a scene in which he crowds close to the camera. "If other people die, I laugh. Death amuses me. I'm bad. Ain't nobody going to get me." It is a moment of hubris: he died soon after, while in police custody—injuries from a beating, my father told me. I remember that we were outraged by the failure to get him medical care. I could visualize him lying comatose on the floor of his cell, dying. And yet that wasn't the worst of it. What I did not know till I began researching this essay was that he was awaiting trial at the time for the murder of a woman thrown from the clubhouse roof one night during a party. I don't know if my father was representing him on that case, though I assume so; he may have found it too disturbing to mention. To become characters in our story, the Angels always required some editing.

The films were finally released in 1983, but by then my father's connections to the Angels were waning, primarily because of his own legal troubles. Nobody wants a lawyer who is in trouble with the law. Years later, while living on my own in Brooklyn, I stopped by my parents' apartment and found my father slumped in a chair, his chin on his chest. My mother stood beside him. "Your father went to see the Hells Angels," she said, "and they weren't very nice to him."

It had been years since he'd been down to the clubhouse. His law license had been suspended, and he had just gotten it back and was trying to rebuild his practice at an age when most people are thinking about retirement. The problem was that Vinnie was dead and Sandy Alexander was in prison on a long stretch for drug dealing.

"Somebody yelled at him to get the fuck out," my mother said. My father's head fell lower.

Sandy Alexander was at my father's funeral. I saw him there in my parents' living room, not at all different from when I was a boy, except he was in a jacket and tie. I hadn't seen him in a long time. He'd been released from prison in 1994 and looked, well, surprisingly great: trim, fit, his hair still black and long, still with a goatee. He was in a black sports coat and tie, gray slacks, white shirt, very appropriate. I had only seen him in biker attire before that.

"To be a Hells Angel back then was the best thing in the world," he said to me. "We owned the night." His eyes were suddenly like little black disco balls, and I remember my father telling me years before that he had gone insane in prison. "We ruled the streets. I knew a woman who was a German countess," he said, mentioning a name I didn't know. "We'd drop acid and go to the Electric Circus and I'd wear jodhpurs and riding boots up to my knees, polished like mirrors, and I'd carry a riding crop." He made a sharp motion with his hand, whipping the air, and laughed in a kind of malevolent, haunted-house way. "Your old man, he understood, he got it all."

And then, just as suddenly, the princely hauteur was gone. He looked worried, at moments even frightened. He said he lived in Queens and was working as a dishwasher, he had heart trouble, he was taking all sorts of medication, there was something about his urine—he had the anxious self-absorption of the frail. He seemed broken more than anything else, and that seemed to me a perfectly natural response to life.

Self-Portrait on Acid

"So what do you think?" asked my mother, looking at the painting on the wall with quiet excitement. "He calls it his self-portrait on acid."

I was probably eight or nine years old. We were in our living room, and the painting, which was a brand-new addition, now dominated the space—a six-foot-tall figure of a man outlined in splattery black strokes, with red and white drips running down like raindrops on glass. The man looked like one of the crazy people we sometimes had to avoid on the street: big zonked-out circles for eyes, empty at the center, and a drugged expression on his face. But there was something more: he had a pendant around his neck, a triangular piece of canvas hanging from a real chain; inside that triangle was a second face, contorted in terror and sorrow.

The picture was by my mother's friend John Glykos, who would drop acid with the Hells Angels at their clubhouse on Third Street and then run back to his studio to paint. He was a Greek merchant seaman who had jumped ship to become an artist in New York. When I think of him now, decades later, it's a picture of him stirring a pot of octopus stew on a little stove while smoking marijuana amid the canvases and wooden stretchers.

My father's clients talked about LSD a lot, how it was going to make the world a more loving and peaceful place, and my mother and I believed this without question because they were his clients and we loved them. But at the same time, I couldn't understand how any of that was going to happen. The mind seemed dangerous to me. I hated the dark, had bad dreams, tried to fend off sleep as long as I could. I didn't want John Glykos staring out from the living room wall, looking terrified at what he was going to do to himself, or maybe to somebody else—maybe even to us. But I didn't want to fail my mother's high standard of artistic appreciation, either. Hand to chin, the pose of thoughtful contemplation I had learned from her in museums, I stared at the painting, wondering how I could avoid letting her down. "I love it," I said. "It's beautiful."

PSYCHEDELIA

IT WAS A COUPLE of years after my father died that my mother told me about the acid trip they took together, the one that made her briefly insane. We were in my living room in North Carolina and she seemed torn between telling it as an amusing anecdote from the early years of her marriage and as something darker, an injury, perhaps a betrayal. "We went to a party in the Village," she said, "very glamorous, full of fascinating people. We got glasses of punch from a bowl on a table and the next thing I knew I was flat on my back on the floor and the ceiling was spinning." She gave an unhappy, theatrical laugh.

"Nobody warned you?" I asked.

"We lay in bed for days. Eventually your father managed to get up, but I still couldn't move. I was in pieces."

That made me think for a second. "How old was I?"

"Maybe five." My mother stopped and looked at me, her eyes hooded, self-protective. She seemed to want me to say something, but I had a dim awareness that this story was no longer about an acid trip, that it was about something else, something I might not want to consider. Without saying a word, I went and got a broom and started sweeping the floor with great concentration, keeping my head down. The image of my parents flat on their backs, out of their minds—it made me frightened, queasy.

My mother sat down on the couch and picked up a book, her way of acknowledging that she had said too much. I went upstairs and called my sister, Perrin. It turned out she'd heard the story already, a few days earlier. "Does that sound possible to you?" she asked. "A punch bowl full of acid and nobody in the room tells them it's spiked?"

"You think they knew?" I asked, startled.

"They knew."

I fell silent. She was right, I could see that instantly, even if everything in me pulled in the other direction.

"Mom told me she fell so deep into herself she couldn't climb out," Perrin said to me. "You're the only reason I came back," Mom had told her. "I looked into your eyes and decided I had to come back and take care of you."

"Who *was* taking care of me?" Perrin had asked her.

"Why, me, of course."

"But who was feeding me?"

"You were a baby, you were still breastfeeding."

"Mom, the LSD would have been in your breast milk, so I must have been tripping, too."

"Ah, that would explain some things."

I listened to Perrin describe their conversation, running one hand nervously over my forehead. There were definitely many things I remembered from that age: my mother's cat-eye sunglasses, the red snowsuit my brother insisted on wearing, even in the summer. It felt odd to me that I couldn't recall something as momentous as our parents' complete psychic collapse.

After hanging up, I sat for a while, trying to reconstruct what it must have been like to be marooned in a tiny apartment high in the sky with your parents tripping. I tried to picture them sprawled in their bed, unable to get up. Would it have looked like sleep to me back then, at the age of five? In my imagination, that sleep went on and on, even when I tried to shake them awake, even when I shouted in their ears. My brother and I must have gone to the kitchen to feed ourselves. We must have gotten on chairs and climbed onto the kitchen counter so we could reach the food in the cabinets. We watched a long unfurling river of TV. When night came and the windows went black, we crawled into our parents' bed to sleep between those big bodies, so familiar to us that they were like extensions of our own.

The more I rehearsed this scenario, the more it felt like an idea, an imaginative reconstruction, not a memory. And then I remembered something I had not thought of for a very long time, a night from around the same age when my father took me to the emergency room with an ear infection. The side of my head throbbed and I was hot with fever, but there was another father-son pair in the big waiting room, and the son, a teenager, was staring at something and talking in a way that seemed strange, heedless. His father stood behind him with a hand on his shoulder, crying.

I had never seen an adult cry before. Tears falling down a grown man's face—it seemed impossible. Father and son were right next to each other, touching, but the son couldn't see or hear his father. It was like they were in two different rooms.

"LSD," my father said, putting an arm around my shoulder and pulling my face into his chest so I couldn't watch anymore.

The warmth of his body, the scent of his shirt: forty years later, I can still conjure those sense memories instantly, vividly. They are real.

There was a part of me that wanted to let my mother's story drop and be forgotten, but the next day, I found myself still circling, unable to veer away. "Did you really not know what was in those drinks?" I asked her.

She was sitting on our beat-up blue couch, the one with all the cat hair on it, dressed in a black satin pants suit and heavy gold jewelry, looking wary and vulnerable. "What do you mean? Of course not."

"It just sounds so awful for no one to warn you."

"Maybe your father knew." She seemed angry, but I wasn't sure whether it was at him or me; she avoided looking me in the eye. "He must have known. He handed me a glass and said, 'Here, drink this.'" She stalked off, and I went upstairs and called Perrin again.

"Does that sound like him?" asked Perrin.

"No." The man I knew was erratic, reckless, but never intentionally mean.

"She blames him for everything, doesn't she?"

"Including dying," I said.

Perrin gave a long sigh, and I could hear her mind shifting in another direction. "She hated when he ran out the door, it made her so mad."

This was a prominent part of our childhood: the phone would ring, he'd answer, and then throw on his coat and dash out, gone for the rest of the night to deal with this or that incredibly urgent but somewhat vague client emergency. In the morning, he'd be sprawled out on the couch in his underwear, a magazine over his face.

"Do you think he, you know, partied?" I asked Perrin. The thought shouldn't have been that surprising—the clients were drug dealers—but it surprised me, left me tight and a little out of breath.

"Maybe," said Perrin. "I don't know. Who can say now?"

I began rubbing my forehead again, in that newly acquired nervous gesture. "He was a teetotaler." *Teetotaler* was the slightly fusty word he always used. He said that over and over again, and it seemed true: if we went somewhere and someone insisted on giving him something alcoholic, he'd ask for Harveys Bristol Cream Sherry and leave most of it untouched. I'd reach over when no one was looking and take a sip. That thick sweet musty syrupy cough medicine taste: to me, that was *him*.

"He was a mysterious person," said Perrin.

My mother's visit came to an end a couple of days later and I was left with her story in all its improbable weirdness. Weren't we the least likely family to almost end in a case of child endangerment?

My parents were lawyers, for god sakes, loving, kind, careful. I had a roomful of books and toys. I went to private school. We played across the street in Gramercy Park, which is private, as my mother told us over and over again—marveling, perhaps, over how far she'd come from her childhood in Brooklyn. You needed a key to get in, and you only got the key if you lived in one of the elegant old buildings facing the park. Yet as I circled those simple facts, a voice just a little altered from my own argued the other side, pointing to a different set of facts:

—Your father was a criminal defense attorney. He represented drug dealers.

—That was just his work; he kept a strict separation.

—The clients came over to the house all the time. The family went out to dinner with them. They picked you up at school when your father got held up in court.

—We didn't try to *act* like them.

—Your mother would talk about how *interesting* they were.

—*Interesting* for her was the opposite of ordinary, that's all. We had a definite fear of being ordinary.

—She would repeat conversations about the higher significance of psychedelics, how they were going to take humanity to the next level of evolution. [Switch to her voice, now audible in my head]: *I'm not saying I agree, but he has a coherent theory . . .*

—Again, that fear of being ordinary.

—You'd think she'd avoid the whole subject after having had such a terrible experience.

—We sometimes skipped over contradictory patches of experience.

—There was the big scary painting hanging in the living room.

—John Glykos's self-portrait on acid. He was a painter friend of my parents.

—You stood in front of that painting when she was yelling at you about your brother, the morning after *he* dropped acid.

—I was too upset to notice the painting.

But I remembered the moment itself with absolute clarity: the odd blankness that filled me as I stood in front of my mother that morning, the living room full of bright morning light, strangely quiet, no radio, no TV. A little bit of that silence was still inside me even now, forty years later, a sort of numb coldness. I could feel it under my skin.

I began rubbing my forehead.

My brother was fourteen when he dropped acid. He did it at a party in the neighborhood and was carried home in the middle of the night by some friends. Our mother answered the door and found him lying in the hall, unable to stand up, hallucinating. Our father took him to the emergency room, the two of them becoming, in essence, a re-creation of the father-son pair I had seen so many years before in that same ER. By the time they got back home, he was speaking a little more coherently. He said that he hadn't taken anything, that someone must have spiked his drink. (Of course, this is the exact same explanation our mother used in my living room in North Carolina, maybe the generic one. Or is it possible that she decided to borrow it from him?)

I didn't actually see any of what I am describing here: my mother told it to me the morning after. What I actually remember from that night are my eyes opening in the dark of my bedroom, and moments later, a polite knock at the front door downstairs, followed by a single agonized wail. It sounded nothing like my brother, but I knew it was him, and in a purely instinctive choice, I decided to retreat back into sleep, where I would be safe.

In the morning, I went downstairs and found my mother standing in her nightgown, agitated. "For him to do this to us," she said. "Despicable, selfish, stupid, cruel." Her voice grew more self-conscious and theatrical as she went on, as if she were addressing a big audience from a stage. "Your father wanted a son, not a client."

Those words made me feel as if I had crossed the line in tandem with him, somehow. I went back up to my room and sat on my bed in an agony of guilt and shame, running over the facts as she had given them to me, trying to make myself feel better. If someone had put the LSD in his drink, he—*we*—were innocent victims, I concluded; that was the most important thing to remember. Of course, this also meant there were people out there who would poison you with LSD if you weren't on your guard. It would be so simple to do, and you would never be able to stop it; except for one sickening moment at the very beginning, you wouldn't even know what had happened to you. The whole world would just suddenly disappear and be replaced with . . . I thought of the terrible wail I'd heard in the middle of the night, the sorrow it carried inside itself.

I ran over these thoughts again and again for the rest of the day, picturing a hand with a dropper putting LSD into a can of soda, then imagining my brother on the floor, his face contorted in anguish. By nightfall, I'd burned myself out and fallen into an exhausted, dreamless asleep. The next morning, I opened my eyes and found that my room was gone: walls, ceiling, carpet, shelves, replaced with a single flat expanse of the color red. My heart began hammering so hard it felt as if the muscles in my chest were tearing. I couldn't breathe. At the same time, a single thought streaked through my mind: *This is what he saw.*

A moment later, I shifted my head and the pillow fell off my face. My room became my room again, with its blue carpet and wooden bookshelves. I sat up, trembling. The pillow in its red case tumbled to the floor.

It was a Monday. At school, I reviewed the moment over and over again, trying to figure out its meaning. What had happened to my brother had almost happened to me. The evidence wasn't the pillow, it was the arterial gush of fear, and the terrible cry I'd heard that night. If I didn't want that to happen to me I would have to be careful, incredibly, fanatically watchful. At lunch, I looked at my sandwich and threw it away.

That night, I examined my dinner for signs of tampering. The more I scrutinized the chicken, the string beans, the water in my glass, the harder it was to tell if they were safe. I had never looked at a chicken breast so closely and had no idea what was normal. That tiny irregularity in the surface could be nothing, or it could be the after-mark of a syringe, cleverly used to inject LSD into the meat. And yet we were at home, my mother had cooked the meal, and the five of us were sitting together at the big round table in our usual configuration, familiar and comforting. I searched my brother's face for evidence of change, the marks of the drug, but saw nothing; my parents were quiet, perhaps a little sad, but at least not angry.

It wasn't till I finished the last of the chicken that I understood my mistake. I started to feel warm, and then a little dizzy. By the time I got back to my room, I was having trouble catching my breath. The walls shimmered, my vision became grainy and dark. I sat down on my bed, then dropped to my back. *It's finally happening*, I thought, a really toxic, grown-up sort of grief beginning to pool at the back of my head. *This is real.*

But it wasn't real. Whatever was in fact happening—a panic attack, I guess—had reached its hidden limit and began to subside. My heart, which had been trying to slam itself open, held together, slowed; my lungs filled with air; I watched the normal world seep back in: the old wool blanket with the fraying edge, the wooden nightstand ... even as a part of me wondered if it wouldn't be better to get it over with already, once and for all. The waiting was now the worst part.

In the weeks that followed, I learned the rules that would let me avoid false alarms: examine food slowly, till you are fully satisfied. If something is unusual, cut it away and throw it out. Better yet, throw out the whole piece. Eat from sealed packages whenever possible. Drink from unopened bottles. Listen for the crack of the seal breaking, the hiss of the air leaking out. If you do not hear those things, throw the bottle away. Do not leave food unattended. Better yet, stare at it until you've finished eating. Make sure no one else touches it, or gets too near it. And leave some food unfinished on the plate, so the police can test it afterward and exonerate you.

But there were so many potential situations that the rules kept branching, multiplying: someone bumped into me on the subway, and I realized my mouth was open. I clamped it shut, my hand flew to my lips, but it was too late. I needed to get home before the worst began to happen. The problem was that the station was packed, and I marched in slow lockstep with the dense mass of people moving down the tunnel, even as I felt the telltale rush of blood to my head, the dizziness.

That night, I tried to stay awake as long as I could, because in the hours since getting off the subway I'd figured out what should have been obvious from the start: my mouth fell open when I was asleep, too. In fact, I was pretty much defenseless when I was asleep, even if my mouth *wasn't* open—even if I taped it shut with packing tape (which I actually tried and rejected). And when I thought about that problem, lying there with the radio playing, my siblings in their bedrooms across the hall, my parents downstairs, the idea of getting dosed with LSD and going insane while I was asleep seemed lonelier than anything else I could imagine, just like that father and son in the ER, trapped in their separate rooms, invisible to each other. Asleep, dreaming, I wouldn't even *know* I'd gone insane. I'd be locked in a dream forever, thinking it was real.

I started to nod off, so I got out of bed and went downstairs, walking back and forth in the living room to stay awake, back and forth past the shadowy furniture.

"What's going on?" It was my mother in her white nightgown, almost glowing in the otherwise dark room.

I stopped. "Nothing."

"What are you doing up?"

A part of me wanted to tell her everything, to let it all rush out, but another part understood just how incredibly humiliating it would be, how crazy it would look. I couldn't even say who was trying to poison me, or why—or why it kept *not* happening. I had no proof, other than that one despairing cry. She looked at me oddly, and I suddenly realized that I was shaking hard, almost rattling.

"What's the matter?" she asked.

"I don't know." I wrapped my arms around myself, trying to hold still.

"Are you sick?"

"No, I'm fine."

She studied me carefully for a long time. "Are you in love?"

It took a moment to figure out what she meant; it was just so oddly out of phase, such a strange choice of non-sequitur; it left me outraged for years afterward. But in that moment, the trembling got worse, became waves of shuddering. My teeth clattered together. It was so hard to speak that I could only whisper a few scattered words, like the clues to an acrostic.

"I see," she said, listening with great concentration. "You mean you're afraid that what happened to him will happen to you."

I nodded, even though hearing it said that way made it seem almost made up, a story or mental construct, the painted backdrop to a play.

"I'll call Mr. Borell in the morning," she said, naming her psychoanalyst.

I tried to stand up straight without shaking. "Not necessary," I said. "I'll be fine."

"Well, let's just see."

And that was enough, somehow. The trembling subsided. I went up to bed and slept, and in the morning, my brother came up to me for the first time since his acid trip. "Mom said I should talk to you," he said.

The truth is that we were not generally friends at this point, though we had shared moments of closeness in the past. Why else would he have been at the center of my convoluted, hysterical thoughts? Why else would I have confused the two of us, as if we were shadow images of each other? There was some kind of bond, clearly, perhaps dating back to our parents' acid trip, when we had spent days and nights watching TV in a world empty of grown-ups.

Now we stood side by side; he was facing one way, me the other, the two of us avoiding eye contact. "Mom told me that you're afraid that someone will put LSD in your food," he said.

I nodded, too emotional to speak. It sounded so stupid, so weird.

"Believe me, that's never going to happen."

"But it did happen."

He gave a snort. "Just think about it for a second, why would anybody waste their expensive drugs on you?"

I got his point right away, of course—that the story we had been sharing, the story I had adopted so fiercely as my own, was just a bullshit excuse. I got it, and yet for some reason I couldn't hold on to it; in another second, the insight was gone.

"What was it like?" I asked.

I glanced over at him. His face contorted as if he were suddenly about to cry, and I realized with horror how fragile he was, that the memories hadn't left him yet. "There was a doll with no eyes," he said, and then bolted into his room and shut the door.

THE NEXT DAY, MY mother sent me to see her psychoanalyst, Mr. Borell. His office was in the neighborhood and I walked there by myself, keeping my mouth shut to prevent someone from slipping acid down my throat. Mr. Borell's office would have been the absolute worst place to lose my mind.

I had never met Mr. Borell before, but I had a fully formed picture of him in my head. He had been a part of my mother's conversation for as long as I could remember, the all-seeing, all-knowing character in the story whose job it was to give the final opinion on everyone and everything. This role was a function of his position at the center of our world: many of my mother's friends had become his patients over the years, and he seemed to share with her what he had learned about them. It was as if he sat at the center of some intricate panopticon, taking in all of human folly; my mother was his disciple, the special beneficiary of his astringent wisdom, and I was *her* disciple.

This made me different from my father. "Mr. Borell believes that your father is completely incapable of insight," she said to me once. "That's why he terminated his treatment. It was a waste of time."

And yet it was my father who called Mr. Borell after the acid trip, once he finally managed to get up and saw my mother's condition. She told me this in North Carolina. "Mr. Borell came to the house. I remember him standing by the bed, looking down at me from a great height. 'She may have to be hospitalized,' he said. 'We'll have to start over from scratch.'"

Of course, I had no idea when I went to see him that he had been a part of that earlier story, that there *was* an earlier story. I slumped in a chair, completely focused on not weeping in front of him. He was leaning back behind an enormous desk. "I don't want you saying that you're seeing Nat Borell now, so everything's going to be all right," he told me, referring to himself in the third person. "Nat Borell isn't going to fix you. You're going to fix yourself."

I nodded in tearful silence, convinced that he was a charlatan and I would never get rid of this thing that had attached itself to my mind like a leech.

Yet over the next couple of years, I would find that Mr. Borell was actually right, that I would in fact fix myself—or more exactly, that some form of workable accommodation would take place inside me, in spite of myself. I still examined my food for tampering, but the false alarms started to feel less all-consuming, to the point where one day I found myself almost a little bored: I knew that if I waited, the attack would pass. After that, the attacks started to taper off, so gradually that I can't quite say when the last one took place. I was still careful to drink out of a sealed bottle, but a part of me was learning to hover above my thoughts, watching them happen while not quite participating in their reality.

The way I came to describe the problem: There were two private screening rooms inside of me playing two different but almost-parallel films that diverged at one key point. In one, I am myself, the beloved son of extravagantly caring parents; my world is safe; I am protected. In the other, someone off-screen has slipped LSD into my drink for no clear reason and I am tripping, going insane. Which movie would I rather be in? I have learned to watch the first and avoid the second, but that doesn't mean the second isn't still playing in its little dark theater, or that it doesn't have a certain seductiveness to it. Even now, decades later, I will occasionally pick up a cup of coffee that has been sitting half drunk on my desk all morning, and think, *How do I know?*

It's a deliberate choice not to take a seat and watch the movie.

Smash

By the time I was nine, I walked around with my shoes untied because it was too difficult to bend over and fix them; climbing the monkey bars left me winded. My mother took me to the YMHA to find something that would slim me down. We ended up in a big rec room lined with portable blue mats, watching a judo class. I saw people in elegant white suits throwing each other to the ground in sharp, stinging arcs. Instantly, I recognized a different kind of hunger hidden inside me.

The instructor led me onto the mat, paired me with a kid about my size, and explained how to do a simple hip throw. I yanked the sleeve as he told me to, stepped in, turned, felt the balance catch and tip. That sensation of somebody's body flying over mine: it was like opening the shutters and letting light flood into a pitch-black room.

We were endomorphs, the kind of people who didn't go outside when it was hot. But I took to judo with the same compulsive habits that I'd learned at the dinner table. If we were supposed to do thirty throwing drills, I did forty. It didn't matter that my lungs were burning. I wanted to feel that wheel turn. I wanted to make my partner into a weightless blur. I wanted to see him sprawled on the mat in front of me, helpless. I wanted to smash them all.

CHOKE

When I was sixteen, I choked out Brian Herskowitz. One second he was trying to pull down on my sleeve to reduce the pressure on his neck, and the next he was very quiet, facedown on the mat. I let go and sat back, not sure what to do.

It was the middle of practice; we were in the dojo, the big mat covered with groups of two, all intently grappling for advantage, chokes, armbars, turnovers, hold-downs. But a moment after I sat down, the action around us stopped, as if by telepathic signal. People disentangled from each other and looked over as they did when someone got hurt in a particularly gruesome way. Sensei came over and turned Brian onto his back. Brian's eyes were closed but he seemed to be . . . not sleeping, exactly—weirder. My memory is that there was some drool. His eyelids twitched.

"*Ii shime-waza na,*" Sensei said. *Good choke.* But his face, usually bemused, was serious.

"He didn't tap," I answered back in English, too shaken to use Japanese.

"He'll be fine."

I was incredibly grateful for those words, even though I believed Sensei was lying. I was already having a bit of an anxiety attack—a spacey unreal feeling, as if it were all happening in a waking dream. I watched the twitching of Brian's eyelids: he was having seizures, I believed, little neurological explosions in his brain, and he was going to wake up *impaired.* And though this was an accident, I knew that I had secretly wished it on him, which made it almost *not* an accident, something I had done on purpose.

Brian woke, sat up.

"Do you want a rest?" I asked, thinking I'd help him off the mat. There was a bench by the windows up at the front, where Sensei kept some of the odd things he found on the street and saved for his sculptures: a dressmaker's mannequin, a foot-high plaster cupid.

"No, I'm good," said Brian, his expression blank. "Keep going." We had been practicing matwork, but he stood up and gripped my collar and sleeve as if we had been doing standwork. Only then did he seem to make sense of what had happened a minute before. "I'm going to get you back," he said suddenly, his mouth curling in a tight-lipped smile.

Sensei, who was standing beside us, laughed; he loved it when things got dramatic. He called out the start of sparring in a loud voice.

We began to move, awkwardly, cautiously. He was four or five years older, and a lot stronger, but too groggy from the choke-out to put a real attack together. I was incredibly relieved by this. We shuffled around in a defensive crouch until the end of practice, and then I hurried off the mat, back through the changing room, and knocked on the door to Sensei's art studio. Inside, his canvases were stacked everywhere: huge, drippy black abstractions that looked something like Chinese characters written at lightning speed, six feet high. He was standing by the table where he ate his meals, a glass of whiskey in one hand. On his head was a big fur hat from the Soviet Union, the gift of some Russian judo players.

With Sensei, the eccentricity only heightened his air of warrior nobility. A friend of my mother had said to me once that he was the most handsome man she had ever seen: high cheekbones, tall forehead, dark eyes that seemed to see and understand everything and always know the right thing to do. The fighter's body, muscled but sleek, was a kind of claim on the world, a form of ownership. Sensei was the only adult I knew who wasn't frightened, or sad, or broken, or afraid of being broken.

"What should I do?" I asked in Japanese.

"Just do that choke again."

Of course, I'd actually meant to ask about Brian, how to make him less mad. "What if he gets me and I tap out?" I asked, hoping for a little reassurance.

Sensei took a sip of his drink and looked at me. "You can't always tap out, Robaato-kun. In Japan, they aren't always going to let you go, either."

"Why not?"

"Tapping out is weak. No one will respect you."

We'd been talking for a while about me going to train at Sensei's old university in Tokyo. In my mind, going to Japan to train was not simply a broadening experience but the imaginative endpoint, a final return to a place I'd never actually been. In Japan, I would become my real self, my Japanese self. That Japanese me would be completely different from my actual self, with its strange loneliness, its worry and sorrow. In Japan, I would join my true tribe, the one I had heard about from Sensei and seen in the photographs in judo books: gigantic shaven-headed thugs who would include me and care about me.

"When I was a kid, we would choke somebody out and wake him up with a kick," Sensei said, sounding nostalgic. "We would choke him out and then when he was still groggy, choke him out again."

"Have you gotten choked out?" I asked.

"Of course. My big brother would choke me out at home. And when I learned a new choke, I would try it out on my little brother."

"You don't think it can hurt your brain?"

He laughed. "The good thing about getting choked out a lot is that you see it's no big deal. You lose your fear. Fear is what gets in the way."

Even on ordinary nights, the trip home from the dojo was melancholy, a long cold return from the heroism and beauty of the mat. But this night, Prince Street was empty and dark, and I walked to the subway alone, past shuttered loft buildings and parked trucks. On the train, I swayed along with everyone else, all the weak, frightened denizens of New York, hugging their briefcases and pocketbooks in their laps. When I walked into the apartment, my father was on the couch in his underwear, eating a bowl of ice cream and watching my mother argue with my brother about his grades. None of them knew that I was about to get brain damaged. I went to my room without a word and lay down on my bed, trying to think and not think at the same time.

A judo choke isn't really a *choke* choke: it doesn't close the airway and stop you from breathing, which means that it won't kill you. It uses the collar of the judo jacket, wrapping it around the neck to apply pressure to the artery and cut off blood flow to the brain. Depending on how deeply *in* the choke is, and how sharply it's applied, blackout can happen almost instantly, or it can require a long drawn-out struggle, a progressive slipping toward darkness. That process is not painful, exactly, not in the way you expect it to be. Your head feels like a balloon filling with air; your vision breaks up and goes black. The defensive moves that might block the choke are simple enough, but you can't remember them.

That's what happened to Brian: he struggled too long, and then slipped into unconsciousness. Nobody could blame me for that, not even him.

The first time Brian ever came to the dojo, Sensei had us work out together the entire time. "Excellent partner for you," Sensei told me in Japanese. "Just the right size, plus a little more experience. If you want to get better, you must try to kill him."

Brian lived in Houston; he came to New York for a couple of weeks at a time to train. During his visits, we worked together so much that I had begun thinking of him as my *sempai*, or senior. In the Japanese way of doing things, *sempai* help train *kohai*, juniors. It is a very Japanese idea, layered with notions of obedience, self-sacrifice, tradition. In Japan, I'd read, *sempai* and *kohai* remain friends their entire lives; I'd seen Sensei's *sempai* come through the dojo when they visited America, seen the natural ease they all had with each other, the intimacy and trust. At times, I would visualize the arrangement as a sort of geometric pattern in which everyone in the judo world was connected: everybody was somebody's *sempai*, and everybody was somebody's *kohai*, and nobody was alone.

When Brian came in for a throw, he would punch me in the neck or smash me in the ear. If he got the throw, he would follow me down to the mat, pressing his knee into my stomach. Once on the mat, he would drill his knuckles into my neck to force my chin up so he could get the choke in, and then he would saw back and forth over my windpipe for maximum hurt, till he got bored and let me go. I loved it. The *sempai-kohai* thing was mostly pretty disappointing in our dojo—Americans seemed constitutionally incapable of thinking about anyone but themselves—but in Brian I had a real Japanese-style *sempai*, someone who cared. Why else would he punch me in the mouth when coming in for a throw? As his loyal *kohai*, I was going to get up and smash him flat to the mat so he would be proud of me. I wanted to destroy him so Sensei would see that I was superior. Because deep down I really hated Brian: hated his fist in my ear and his knee in my stomach, hated his knuckles digging into my jaw.

So really, you could argue that choking him out was just *on-gaeshi*, the grateful return of the obligation owed to a caring *sempai*. Exhausted, I finally fell asleep.

The next day, at school, I pulled out pen and paper and tried to come up with a plan. Brian tended to lean forward, arms stiff, so he was weaker to the front. I would come in low for the shoulder throw, first to the right, then to the left, where his balance wasn't as good. If I could hold him off till he went home, I would be safe.

The one thing that never occurred to me was simply not going. I had never missed a day in six years. The rhythm of the subway, the run up the five flights of stairs in the old loft building, the changing room, the big mat with its red vinyl covering, the *thwump, thwump* of people getting thrown—to me, that was being alive.

At the dojo that evening, Sensei pulled me over to Brian. "Your partner is waiting," he said.

"You know I'm going to choke you out tonight, right?" Brian gripped my jacket tight. He had that smile again, the corners of the mouth pulled up, the eyes glittering.

I was suddenly filled with a bleak giddiness. "Actually, I'm going to choke you out," I said. "Just like yesterday."

Sensei laughed; Brian smiled harder. "Don't bother tapping," he said.

Even the throwing drills felt different that night, with Brian banging his chest against mine as he came in, punching his fist against my ear. When it was time for matwork, he smiled, drew his finger across his neck like a knife, and then went straight for the choke. And when sparring started, he didn't even bother trying to throw, just grabbed my lapels and yanked me down onto all fours, into a standing choke—wrapping my jacket around my neck while pinning my head between his knees. I got out of that, got out of everything, but every time Sensei called out a switch of partners, Brian grabbed my sleeve again, refusing to let me go—until suddenly practice was over, and I was sitting on a bench in the changing room, trying to breathe, so deeply tired that I couldn't hold up my head.

"Tomorrow," said Brian, walking over to his bag.

WRITING IS MY WAY of remembering. The physical act of putting words down on paper forces me to create a meaningful sequence, a narrative that can arc through time. In the process, I remember all sorts of unpleasant stuff that I had previously pruned from the official record, the version I tell myself in bed at night while falling asleep. This is a way of saying that Brian wasn't really the first person I ever choked out, that the first was a guy by the name of Angel, and that I choked him out not once but twice. On purpose.

To tell this part of the story, I need to jump back to when I was fourteen. I'd moved from the kids' class, where choking wasn't allowed, to the adults', where it was constant, a killjoy. As I tugged on my opponent's collar, trying and failing to find the point of maximum torque, choking seemed like a long hot dirty slog, boring and stupid. And getting choked—there was nothing good about getting choked. It was like being at the bottom of a pit and watching someone fill in the dirt. It was better not to even think about it, just tap out right away.

And then one night I was partnered with Sensei during matwork practice; he kept getting the choke, and I kept tapping out. "You need to protect your neck better," he said to me in Japanese. "It's about time you learned."

"I'm trying," I said.

"You need to try harder."

He went straight for the choke again, maneuvering himself on top of me so we were face-to-face, our noses just an inch apart. "It's sleepy time," he said, sawing his wrist over my windpipe. "Time to go to sleep." I whimpered a little, he snapped the choke closed, and I sputtered and flailed as if I were drowning, pounding the mat with my hand. "Pull down on my sleeve, make space," he said, but a part of me refused to give in and listen, and I just kept slapping the mat. He released his hold, and I gasped, as if coming up for air. But it was a trick. "Say nighty-night," he cooed in my ear, and then pulled the choke closed again.

We went back and forth like that, as if opening and closing a spigot of despair. Finally, he let me go and I kneeled and started to retie my belt, which had come loose. Tears were in my eyes. I stood up, legs shaky. *Gratitude*, I told myself. *Kansha*. Sensei was going to make me stronger.

I started paying attention when the class lined up in pairs on the mat to practice chokes, experimenting on each other's necks. A year or so later, I went to a competition and choked six kids into submission with the exact same technique, one after the other. I would see the opening, slip in the choke, *snick*, wait for the kid to tap out. After the last time, I glanced over to see Sensei standing on the sidelines, laughing. "Well done," he said in Japanese, the words sounding so beautiful in that harshly lit public space.

"Thanks for all your help," I said, bowing. *This is the feeling that winners have*, I thought to myself, though it seemed to be happening not so much inside as *near* me: a total momentary absence of fear, as startling and strange as those rare moments in New York when the street noise suddenly stops.

I rode back with Sensei and the other kids from the dojo, packed into his ancient little car, which used a length of clothesline as a pull-rope to operate the window wipers. The trophy was at my feet, a sort of miniature war monument, if war monuments were made out of oddly shaped bits of wood and plastic, one layer piled on top of the other. At the top was a golden judo man, standing at attention. I treated it with ironic disdain, secretly in love with it.

When I got home, the lights were all off; I could feel the emotion hanging in the shadows, a deep hopeless sorrow. My father was the only one there, on the couch with the radio on and a glassy look on his face, the expression he got when he felt depressed—one of the periodic negatives of being a brilliant criminal defense lawyer, we all believed. I put the trophy in my room and then came back out and sat down. "What's the matter?" I asked. There was no point in mentioning the competition; nothing about that part of my life interested my parents.

"It used to be all marijuana dealers," he said. "They were peaceful and fun. If you lost, the jail time wasn't too bad. But now it's cocaine, and they can get twenty years to life."

"That's their fault, not yours."

"The clients are different, too, violent people. They'd kill you as soon as look at you."

The clients had always been a little scary, it seemed to me—bikers, self-destructive daredevils, the kind of counterculture types who liked guns. My father had been blithely unaware up till now, perhaps a little bit in love. "Did something happen?" I asked.

"I think I might lose this case."

We went out to get something to eat. He wasn't wearing a shirt, just a windbreaker zipped to the top. Shoes with no socks, the laces trailing. I hadn't had time to shower after the competition, so my hair was matted with sweat. Yet it didn't surprise me that he drove us to Peter Luger's in Brooklyn—at times like these, he wanted steak, and he wanted it to be big and expensive. Walking inside, I knew we would stick out and they would treat us badly in all the ways that restaurants in New York can. My father ordered the steak for two—an obscenely large slab—and then pretty much ate it himself in a kind of accelerating frenzy, forgetting fork and knife and picking it up with his hands. And then he put the bone down and with glistening fingers pulled a pack of cigarettes out of his pocket.

"Dad, you can't smoke here," I said.

He arched his eyebrows and lit a cigarette, inhaling deeply and then blowing the smoke out of his nose. "I'm not bothering anyone."

"They're going to come over."

"I'm a paying customer."

The waiter was at our table a moment later. "You can't smoke here," he said, blunt. "You know that."

In moments like these, there was always an anxiety that we would end up being utterly humiliated. It was a low-level fear that never quite went away. I braced myself as my father glanced up at the waiter, but he just stubbed out the cigarette and went back to his inwardness, a kind of bleary trance. Our cheesecakes came and we ate them in about two seconds, paid the check, and got up to go, stumbling for the door. It was as if there were a hole in my chest, and the blackness were pouring in, and I was choking on it.

Afterward, at home, I lay on my bed, unable to remember the way it felt to make those kids tap out—the way choking them into submission seemed to make me levitate above the rest of the world. I glanced over at the trophy that sat on the floor by my bed, and it didn't even look like cheerful, ironic junk anymore, just ordinary junk.

And yet I really had won.

At the dojo a few weeks later, Sensei called me over to show me a letter from the U.S. Judo Federation: my first-place finish had gotten me into the regionals in Chicago. "Six chokes in a row," he said, laughing with pleasure. "And now you can go and choke another six, and nobody will see it coming."

Normally, I would have wanted nothing more than to celebrate with glasses of whiskey in the studio, to sit and talk about which throws to use, and when to apply the choke, and draw comfort from his certainty that the world was safe, that I was like him, a wolf, not a sheep. But what I felt now was an anxious churning deep in my stomach, so painful that I couldn't pretend. I knew that if I went to Chicago, I would lose.

"I don't know, it's really far," I said. "Plus, right now, I've got lots of schoolwork."

He looked genuinely puzzled at this. "You don't want to go?"

"No, I want to go," I said, reversing. "I'm going to go."

I traveled with my mother, who on the day of the tournament disappeared into the stands gripping a novel by Colette, looking slightly shaken by her surroundings. The competition space was vast, bigger and scarier than anything I'd seen up to that point. The endless gymnasium covered in mats, ten or twelve matches going on at the same time, the noise, the people, the bleachers, the fluorescent lights, the waiting: it gave me a pulsing sick headache that seemed to expand and contract with my breathing. Suited up and ready to go, I paced back and forth on shaky legs, trembling; then, as my first match finally drew near, my opponent walked up to me with his coach. "Look," the coach said to him, putting a hand on his shoulder. "He's afraid of you, he can't even look you in the eye." I was just two feet away but he talked as if I couldn't hear him, and so it felt as if I were eavesdropping on some essential knowledge about myself. Instantly, I averted my eyes, terrified. Just then, our names were called; we stepped onto the mat and bowed, and a moment later he had me in a choke: I felt the familiar pressure in my head, the flash of panic. I tapped out.

Back in New York a few days later, I pounded up the stairs to the dojo, opened the door, and saw the red mat glowing in the darkened space; the throwing dummy slumped against the wall; the big vertical pipe in one corner, wrapped in an old mat for protection. The electric lights were off, but sunlight slanted through the big windows at the front. It was a Tuesday, which meant that there was no kids' class, and it was still way too early for the adults to arrive. Sensei was out. An in-between time. I changed and lay on the mat in my judo suit, staring at the piece of calligraphy that hung on the wall, four Chinese characters rendered in strong black strokes like judo players tangled in combat: *Use All Your Power for Righteousness.*

I would have to train much harder, I believed, to make up for what had happened in Chicago.

And then the door to the stairway opened and Angel entered. I hated working out with him. He was big, fat, awkward, immovable, always kicking me in the shins and stomping on my toes. I had no idea how old he was: he seemed like a gigantic kid, but there was heavy stubble on his cheeks. He wore his hair in a bowl cut, and when he took off his glasses, you could see that one of his eyes was a little bit droopy. I couldn't think of him as either *sempai* or *kohai*, senior or junior.

We ended up practicing chokes, one sitting and the other applying the technique till the first one tapped out. He started and then it was my turn. "Right spot?" I asked.

"Almost. Yeah, that's it."

I released him and he sat up, rubbing his neck. The dojo was dark and still, empty. There was a long pause, and I had that feeling that I sometimes couldn't avoid—loneliness like a draft through a crack in the wall, even here—the feeling that would always drive me to practice harder.

"You can choke me out if you want," he said.

"What do you mean?"

"It's okay, I like it," said Angel. "I get choked out all the time at my other club in Brooklyn."

I stopped and looked at him: the heavy round face, the stubble, a slightly droopy eye, hair in a bowl cut. For the first time, I wondered if he might be simple. "It kills brain cells," I said.

"Who cares? It feels good."

It seemed totally illicit and creepy and wrong, but I already knew I was going to do it, could already see myself doing it, as if there were really no other choice. I put him into a choke and instead of increasing the pressure slowly, as I normally did, snapped it tight. I felt him go limp, and then I got up and rolled him to his back.

Angel looked asleep in a sort of untidy way, eyes half open, showing the whites, mouth slack. He gave out a couple of alarming snores and I shook him and then his body fluttered a little bit, his legs began to kick. I started to panic, but then his eyes opened. I helped him sit up. His head hung loose.

"Are you okay?" I asked.

"Don't worry."

"What's it like?"

"A little like you're drunk." He shook his head to clear it. "You can do it again if you want."

I did, as if doing it again might erase the first time.

Brian was serious about choking me out; he kept at it, day after day, through full-out battles that seemed to last the whole class. But we were reasonably chummy in the changing room afterward. "I can't believe you got away again," he said, pulling on his jeans.

"Yeah," I said, hands so dead I had trouble untying the drawstring of my judo pants. "That was a good one."

"But I'm going to get you tomorrow. You know that, right?"

"Yeah, well, we'll see."

At home, I would lie in bed, so tired I couldn't keep my eyes open, yet unable to fall asleep—body aching on what felt like the deep cellular level, feet twitching from excess tension. Floating in the dark on the edge of consciousness, I would imagine myself getting choked out, as if I were watching a film clip: Brian letting go of my collar, standing up to take a look; me spread out on the mat, legs kicking ever so slightly in reaction to the little seizures taking place in my brain. The thought was so deeply, poignantly sad that it brought tears to my eyes.

During the day, I did everything with an intense nostalgia, as if for the last time. This might be the last time I hung out with my father at the diner on the corner, listening to his stories about the clients and their violent, drugged-out antics, the two of us laughing away our unease. The last time I sat in a restaurant with my mother, listening to her catalog my father's failings, her disappointment a kind of passionate dark aria. Always in the back of my mind was the knowledge that I'd have to be at the dojo later, that I'd have to fight harder than I knew how, and that if Brian got me, I would never learn Japanese or go to Japan or go to college. I would wake up and be Angel.

"I don't think he's ever leaving," Sensei said to me in Japanese that night, laughing. It was the middle of practice and we were standing on the mat with Brian, all three of us dripping with sweat, retying the belts that held our jackets closed. Sensei had a point: I'd lost count, but it seemed way past when Brian normally left for Houston.

"I'm not afraid of him," I said, though in fact I was more afraid every day, certain that I was dwindling.

"That's good," said Sensei. "Fear is the tallest barrier."

Sensei called out the beginning of sparring, and Brian snagged his iron grip on my jacket. I managed to snap it off and knock him down with a footsweep, and he fell to his butt and got up slowly. "That's it," he said, with that awful smile. "You've made me mad."

We danced around for a while, I took a step back, he followed, and I came in for the shoulder throw and flipped him cleanly up and over. We both rolled through in a kind of somersault, and then he was clinging to my back and I was protecting my neck as he dug into my throat with his knuckles. Luckily, I'd gotten my hands in place quickly, so he wouldn't be able to get a tight enough grip on the collar to make the choke work. I could coast and catch my breath for as long as he kept trying.

And then I opened my eyes and found myself lying on the mat. The action in the room had stopped, and people were staring. Sensei was looking at me without his usual amusement, a little concerned. I had the confused sense that I had somehow fallen asleep in the middle of the workout. I felt stupid and guilty—what a terrible, unforgiveable thing to do. There was saliva around my chin; I wiped it with my hand. And then I jumped up, suddenly frantic. "What happened?" I asked, louder than I meant to, my voice sounding odd—angry. "What happened?"

No English

Once I finally made it to Japan, I spent a couple of months doing judo but gave it up: the world outside of the dojo was just too interesting, too marvelous. But that stubborn desire to impose my will transferred to other things, one of which was a complete refusal to speak English—even when the other person's English was better than my Japanese. It might become a long slog, a war of attrition, with that other person speaking in one language and me in the other, but eventually that other person would get worn down and switch.

THE FLOATING BRIDGE OF DREAMS

THE JAPANESE LANGUAGE CLASS met twice a week in a little storefront belonging to a *sumi-e*, or ink painting studio. A couple of large tables, coffee cans full of brushes, scrolls in various states of finish hanging on the walls—a crow on a withered branch, a sprig of cherry blossoms. I was the only kid in a group of grown-ups that included a man with a mustache who fell asleep halfway through the lesson, and a fragile-looking woman who announced that she had just become a Buddhist and then smiled a nervous smile.

We made a circle with our chairs, and the teacher stood in the center. She held her hands in front of her, fingertips touching, and her strange beauty seemed to have something to do with the secret she was going to teach us. "Please listen and repeat," she said. When she spoke next, the sounds moved as quickly as light in the leaves of the trees. I leaned forward till I was almost off the chair, watching her mouth and throat, her hand as she pointed to one thing after another: book, table, clock, lamp, pen.

An hour later, when my parents pulled up in front to pick me up, I came out staggering, light-headed. I could barely pull the car door shut. "How was it?" asked my mother.

"All right," I answered, not wanting to reveal anything, wanting the experience to remain entirely my own.

"We stopped in a bookstore and got you these." She handed me a couple of novels by Yukio Mishima, in keeping with her tendency to forget that I was only twelve years old.

"Tell us what you learned," said my father, who was driving. "Tell us the word you liked best."

I glanced down at my vocabulary sheet and chose the longest and spikiest. "*Wakarimashitaka*," I said. "It means, *Do you understand?*"

Wakarimashitaka. Wakarimashitaka. My father repeated it a couple of times; he prided himself on his ear for languages. Learning Japanese had been his suggestion, a puzzled but hopeful reaction to the judo classes I'd been taking, their strangely disciplined physical mayhem, so alien to a family of pleasure-loving endomorphs like my own. *Rei*, my judo teacher would say, and we would all bow, priestly in our white suits. *Hajime*, and we would start to fight, pulling and twisting, smashing each other to the ground. Neither my father nor my mother understood why anybody would subject themselves to something so uncomfortable, or what all the violence might have to do with me, their sweetly obedient son. They tried to turn it into something that made sense to them, a different sort of self-improvement: learning a language.

"Anyone who can speak to them in their own language will rule the future," said my father, strangely prescient about the rise of the Japanese economy in what was still only 1975. "Who knows where this could take you," he said. "You could end up the first Jewish emperor of Japan."

I set to work on that problem the very next day, after school—or on the problem I thought was that problem, though in fact it was different. Sitting in my room, I closed my eyes and imagined myself in a chair just inches from my teacher, listening to her say each word, repeating it back to her. Chair, book, table. I could see her lips forming the phrases. A kind of dark energy filled my body.

Looking back, can anything be more obvious? I was twelve years old, and desire was still a metaphysical thing. My head told me that there was just one world, and it stayed the same no matter how you described it, but my body knew differently: there were in fact two worlds, English and Japanese, male and female, and the words I was learning were tiny boats to sail me across. When, weeks later, I limped uncertainly through a short conversation in class about the weather—*Ah, Robaato-san likes the rain? I like the rain, too*, she said—it was like a bracelet clicking shut. She had understood me. We had spoken.

The English world wasn't like that. In the English-speaking world, the two halves never quite fit together.

"Your father and I were engaged for years," my mother said to me. "We couldn't break up and couldn't take the leap, so one weekend we just eloped. When I told my parents they were very upset, but eventually my father agreed to put on a big wedding for us."

My mother and I were sitting in Alice Tully Hall in Lincoln Center, waiting for the string quartet to enter, the lights to go down, the concert to begin. Her tone was lofty, as if we were two connoisseurs of human folly, as if we weren't talking about her and my father, and thus about me. I folded my hands on my lap and smiled a completely frozen smile, my thoughts also frozen. It was impossible for me to think beyond my desire not to think.

"So on the day of the wedding," she continued, "I panicked and told my father that I'd changed my mind and didn't want to get married after all. And he said that was a wise decision and he would call and cancel everything, leave it all to him." She laughed very quietly. "You see, I'd forgotten that I was already married."

I nodded and tried to look unruffled.

After the concert, we went out to dinner at the sort of restaurant that was dark and glittering, the food rich and complicated—exactly what my father hated. My mother was eating mussels in wine sauce; she put one on my plate for me to try. "When your father and I were first married, I wanted to impress him with a big home-cooked dinner, the kind of thing he likes. I called him at the office, asked him when he'd be home, and then I cooked two big steaks, baked potatoes, and I waited. And I waited. He was an hour late, two hours late. I called his office, but there was no answer. I decided to eat my steak, and then I looked over at his and decided to eat that too, so it wouldn't go to waste. And then I was so sick to my stomach that I barfed."

"Where was he?"

"Some client thing."

I have a vague memory of snails with butter and garlic: what I liked best about them was the long thin fork that came with them. I made myself busy, not looking up.

When I was listening to my mother, I felt as she felt, even when I didn't want to. But when I stepped outside of her point of view, I immediately went back to loving my father with an extravagant sort of need. I would hang around his office with him after school, listening to him talk with his clients, and then when it got late and the windows went black, he would call home and tell my mother that we were on our way home for dinner, and then go back to talking and somehow forget to leave, until finally everyone in the room agreed that, even though there was more urgent business to discuss, they were all very hungry, and suddenly we were at a table in one of the fish restaurants near the Fulton Fish Market that my father liked when he was trying to lose weight.

I remember walking through the door of one such place with a group of clients and lawyers from my father's firm. "Shouldn't we call Mom and let her know?" I whispered to my father.

"Do you really want to go home and eat your mother's pot roast?"

"Not really," I said.

"Then we're on the same page."

We filled a big table. One of my father's law partners was a skilled magician and did tricks with the breadsticks, making them disappear and reappear in people's clothing in vaguely lewd ways. There was raucous laughter, shouting, many conversations that eventually converged on one low-pitched conversation. "I've got a strategy," my father was saying. "Throwing doubt on the police investigation is the most important thing. It's a frame-up. We were framed. That's the line we're going to follow."

I always liked that sort of wizardry, as if my father could access some magic power inside him and wrap the clients in an invisibility spell that would protect them from harm, from the cruel vindictiveness of the police.

"What about the drugs?" the client asked. He was tall and very thin, I remember, with a bit of a mustache and wispy hair in a little ponytail.

"You guys didn't know the drugs were in the trunk, because the car didn't belong to you. It's registered to that other guy," my father said, and began to laugh, and we all laughed with him, because his laughter was big and exuberant and made us all feel safe and good.

When we got back home, I stood in the living room as my father and mother argued, my mother furious, my father puzzled, defensive. It was work, he told her, you can't always control what happens with work.

"Forget about the dinner I made. You can't get him back so late on a school night."

"He's learning about life," said my father.

I trusted him completely; that feeling was such a deep part of me that I could never change it, even if I wanted to. The sense of mistrust bled out into everything else instead. My eyes would pop open in the middle of the night and I would wonder about the real meaning of things. I would worry about what I had said or what other people had said to me, what they had really meant, until my thoughts raced in circles and my legs twitched and I couldn't go back to sleep.

But the Japanese world was infinitely simple, beautiful, clean:

Is this a book?

Yes, a book.

The subject of conversation hardly mattered. What mattered was saying it in just the right way, with the mouth almost closed and the body in just the right posture of dignified calm, so different from my usual attitude, which was anxious and fidgety, all drumming fingers and bobbing knees. What mattered was listening carefully for the answer and understanding each word. What mattered was the bracelet clicking shut.

Wakarimashitaka. Did you understand?

Hai, wakarimashita. Yes, I understood.

At school, I suffered from a terrible shyness, so self-conscious about what I said and how it might be heard that each word seemed to break apart as I spoke it. Was it the right thing or the wrong thing to say? Would people like it or be angry? Those thoughts spun in my head, even as I was talking; the effect was that I didn't so much talk to anyone as watch myself speak on the TV in my mind, my heart in my mouth in case I inadvertently launched some terrible, irreversible cataclysm.

Instead, I went home and sat at the desk in my room and practiced writing *kana*, the symbols that the Japanese language uses to express sound on the page. Writing *kana* was like drawing tiny images of women, women sitting, standing, walking. Looking at those curving shapes, I could see my teacher standing at the center of our circle of chairs, her hand tracing the shapes of the *kana* themselves on the big pad she used to teach us how to write. "You're getting better," she said when I showed her my practice sheets. "Keep going."

When she decided to move back to Japan, the word *sad* didn't occur to me. It just felt as if something were suddenly out of place, and I had to sit and look out the window, searching among the rooftops. Before she left, I asked her, "How will I know when I'm fluent?"

"You'll dream in Japanese," she said.

Years passed, and I kept waiting for it to happen, flipping through my flash cards every night before going to sleep, writing down my dreams in a notebook each morning. I went to college, majored in Japanese, decided to spend my junior year at a university outside of Tokyo. The idea was to break down the wall between the classroom and the world—the wall that was holding back my fluency, my dreaming.

The problem was that Japan was so far. I was in college, yes, but I called home every night. Just the idea of going to a foreign country thousands of miles away frightened me so much that I couldn't physiologically inhabit the thought: whenever I tried to imagine what living in Japan might be like, my mind went bright white, and a low hum filled my body, as if a wire had come loose inside the TV of my selfhood. The Japanese university application, the airplane ticket—I did all that mechanically, by rote, moving through the glare and the hum. On the day of departure, my father drove me to the airport, the two of us silent, staring straight ahead. My face felt swollen, as if I had walked straight into a wall in the dark. The best I can say is that it felt as if we were on the way to a funeral for someone we both loved dearly but whose name I couldn't remember.

It wasn't till I was on the airplane, waiting for us to push back from the jetway, that it occurred to me that I might be making a mistake. I jumped up and made for the front. "Where are you going?" asked the stewardess. Everyone else was buckled in. She was busy closing things.

"I'm sorry, but I've got to get off," I said simply.

"It's too late, the doors are locked."

My eyes went wide. The frozen sea inside me began to slosh. "No, you don't understand."

"Sit back in your seat. Right now," she said. "We're about to move."

I went back and sat down, and then my mind went white like the blinding light from a naked bulb. I spent the next thirteen hours staring out the porthole at the sky, feeling my own emptiness mirrored there. The sun rose and set a couple of times: reds and yellows that made my head hurt. At Narita Airport, I followed everyone else off the airplane, not clear on where we were going or what I would have to do in order to wake from this stubborn dream. What frightened me most was the way the Roman alphabet had suddenly disappeared from the world. I had never understood how those familiar shapes signified the human voice, and thus human kindness. Signs were in *kanji*, the Chinese characters that look like dinosaur skeletons or the bones of dead birds, curled in on themselves. I'd learned about fifteen hundred *kanji* in school, enough to read a newspaper, but now I couldn't understand a single one. Their voices had closed to me, like doors.

I believed so completely that I was lost that no proof to the contrary could convince me otherwise: not chatting quite successfully in Japanese with the cab driver, my voice a nervous teakettle singing, not sitting in my landlady's parlor, a little plate of sweet bean paste balanced on my lap as we talked in Japanese about my life in the U.S. I understood in a distant, intellectual way that she was kind, but it did not register physically in my body. Instead, my mind kept drifting to the phone booth I had seen from the taxi window, standing incongruously alone at the end of the suburban street, with nothing else but houses and walled gardens around. I wanted to speak to my parents, to hear their voices, but we had agreed that international calls were too expensive. "Don't worry, I'll write every day," my mother had said to me.

"Me too," I said, with the distinct feeling that I was talking about someone else. I still didn't believe that I was really going, though my flight was just a few days away.

Nobody stopped to consider how out of character this bit of economy was for us, given our general tendency to spend like sailors out on a spree. Nobody even bothered to find out how much a long-distance call might actually cost. I remember being confused about why we were so certain on this one odd point, but I couldn't quite formulate the question, let alone speak it out loud.

I said good night to my landlady, and instead of walking over to the little apartment building next door, I headed down the street to the phone booth. When I stepped inside and pulled the folding door shut, the glass enclosure filled with light. Night had fallen, and the neighborhood was dark. I placed my hand on the receiver but did not lift it from the cradle.

The next morning, I got up as early as I could and tried to walk the five blocks to campus from my apartment. As my landlady had explained it, the route was simple, but I somehow managed to get mixed-up. Dead-end alleys, blank cinderblock walls, strange blind corners, and not a single street sign, or a soul to ask for directions: after a couple of hours of wandering and backtracking, I gave up all pretense of figuring out where I was going and just concentrated on putting one foot in front of the other, like a traveler lost in the desert. When by sheer luck I finally stumbled upon my little apartment building and staggered into my room, I had to lie down on the tatami, trembling.

An hour or two later, I sat up and wrote my first letter home:

Dear Family,

I'm here in Japan and everything looks incredibly tiny, like a scale model. My apartment is a single room and I can almost touch both

> walls when I spread out my arms. But there's a big window and the floor is tatami matting and smells like straw, a very sweet smell. I love it.

I filled the sheet and sealed the envelope without ever mentioning that I had just gotten lost for an entire afternoon a block from my house—an experience like almost drowning in a foot of water. I was going to hover above all that: if I didn't admit to being scared, then I wasn't scared. But at the same time, the underlying meaning of my letter was that I was terrified and didn't think I'd last another day.

The neighborhood's little post office was straight down the street, so I walked over and mailed the letter the next morning and then ran back, nervous that my building would disappear. Once inside my room, I didn't leave except to check the mailbox. Every few hours I would creep downstairs to open the little metal container and run my hand around the inside, then climb back to my room. I did this for about two weeks, until I found a letter inside, sitting there very modestly, as if it weren't important. Heart banging hard, I tore open the envelope and pulled out the sheet of yellow legal paper, examined the blue ink, my mother's big, looping script, pressed the sheet to my face and breathed in the papery scent. And then I read:

"Dear Robert," it began, "I'm glad to hear you're settling in." She had gone to the supermarket and bought lamb chops; she'd taken her heels to the shoemaker.

I read it again and again, about a thousand times, at first overjoyed, and then obscurely disappointed in a way I could not understand. This was just a list of trivia. Where was the help I needed? After an hour or two, I felt almost annoyed, vaguely resentful.

I wrote back that afternoon, determined to try again. Classes had started, so I told her about the food in the cafeteria where I ate lunch on campus every day: the bowl of rice, the little dish of brightly colored pickles, the green tea poured from gigantic banged-up teapots the size of a watering can. "Things are off to a great start!" I said. Surely, she would get the message now.

Her reply: "Dear Robert, So nice to hear from you. It's been raining the last few days." She'd gone to the movies; she'd gone to the bank.

Our correspondence continued this way for an entire year. We were nothing if not dutiful, sitting down to write as soon as the other's reply had arrived. I would say something about school, and she would list all the chores she had done that day. Her letters covered exactly one sheet of yellow legal paper, never more, never less. It took exactly seven days to get the next one, but I checked the mailbox every day anyway, the act of peering into the container part of my daily ritual of return.

At times, the sheer flatness of my mother's letters made me suspect that something might be wrong. I would register that feeling for just a moment, in the unthinking way that you notice a drop in the daylight when a cloud moves across the sun. My heart would seize up, my shoulders tense and then relax. But I ignored it, because I didn't really want to know if something was wrong. I was barely managing to get through my day as it was, walking the five mysterious blocks to school and not disappearing.

What I would learn when I returned to New York was that something *was* wrong: my father was in trouble with the law. Later that year, his office would be raided and DEA agents would carry away his records. The process moved with astounding slowness, and formal charges were still a couple of years away, but prosecutors were talking about weapons possession, drug running, drug selling, drug use. The source of these accusations seemed to be a long-time client, so there was an element of betrayal, as well—a sense that the world had been turned upside down and revealed as something different from what we had always thought. We had always thought that being a criminal defense family was really fun and exciting and glamorous because we got to see up close what other people only saw on TV.

My father fell into a deep depression. He stopped going to court and talking to new clients. He stopped going to his office. Current clients began hearing the rumors and leaving. My sister would tell me later that our father went raging through the house one night, saying he was going to call me up and tell me to come home; my mother ran after him, screaming that he better not go near the phone, weeping. My brother removed all the knives from the kitchen: it looked like my father might try to hurt himself.

Though I didn't know it back then, my father's legal problems had actually started *before* I left—which is why, I think, they didn't want me calling from Japan. Letters were better: it was so much easier to say nothing in a letter.

Those letters sit in a box in the attic now: my mother saved mine and gave them back to me when I returned, and I saved hers and kept them. I got the box down the other day and began sorting through them, long enough to find the first couple in the sequence, the ones I've quoted here. But then my hands began to tremble, and it got harder and harder to breathe. I ended up putting them all away, closing the lid, and taking them up to the attic again.

THERE WERE PLENTY OF other foreign students at the university, but they were all grouped together in the dormitories on campus, a self-enclosed pack. I envied them but also chose to avoid them, because I didn't want to speak any English. It had never occurred to me that the alternative would be speaking nothing at all. I was alone much of the day, but I could not shake my loneliness even when I was at school, surrounded by other people. I walked home enveloped in silence, went to bed in that same silence, woke in silence. In that bubble of isolation, my interior life swallowed the rest of me. I was entirely my interior. My interior felt paradoxically huge and also tiny, like a cramped and narrow closet. Going through my day was like watching the world through a peephole bored into the back of that closet, spying on events that were mysteriously fraught with a meaning I couldn't know, a narrative that was always incomplete. Surfaces and stray details became important; the look of the street, the odd scratches on a car in traffic, faces and the clothes people wore. I would think about them in the silence of my little room, still not equipped with TV or radio. *I'm alone* repeated endlessly in my brain, a kind of emergency signal that

I was powerless to turn off. Even though I'd been on my own at college for two years, I hadn't ever learned to truly care about myself: to think that I mattered enough to not disappear when I was alone.

And then one day at the school library a student who needed help with his English homework approached me; I corrected some pages of writing; with Japanese politeness, he invited me home to meet his family. His sister took me to see some of the tourist sights around Tokyo and then introduced me to a friend of hers, who took me to a coffee shop to meet one of her friends, who then invited me to go sightseeing . . . In this way I began a strange, meandering journey from coed to coed, each playing host for a while, until she got tired of talking so slowly and passed me on to one of her friends.

Those outings had some of the feel of dating, but they were really just cultural encounters, a sort of cross-cultural proto-dating. On some level, I understood that I was being treated as a curiosity, but that seemed only natural to me and I never resented it. Isn't that what the opposite sex is, at least at the beginning? A fascination, a hunger to know, an electric strangeness? Isn't that what travel is? Foreignness? We sat in coffee shops and stared at each other across not one but two barriers, gender and culture, even as those two barriers blurred together and became one.

The good thing was that I didn't have to agonize about what to say, as I had back in the U.S. Speaking in Japanese demanded my complete attention; there was no energy left over for self-consciousness. Just stringing a series of grammatically correct sentences together felt as if I were steering a gigantic ship in difficult waters.

The women would ask me question after question. What did my father do? How many siblings did I have? Where did I go to college? In Japan, government and the most prestigious corporations draw from the top universities only. When I said *Harvard*, the coeds' eyes went wider; for the first time, Harvard seemed not a burden of expectation but something of value—it surprised me, because I'd never thought of it that way. But now I could see them suddenly lean forward across the table in the coffee shop. We were a little bit closer, to the point where I could almost imagine what it might be like to touch their hands. And then it would come out that I was Jewish, and they would lean a little closer still. Of course, that's why you're so smart, they would say. Is your family very rich?

Now wait a second, I said, the first time I heard this. It seemed like the opening to a Philip Roth novel. But I soon came to see that the stereotype was a complete positive for them, that nothing was intended but admiration. Rich, connected, smart: those were all *good* things.

"They say that Jews are the foreigners most like the Japanese," one girl said to me. "They value family and education."

"That's true," I answered, reasoning that this exactly summed up my own family, the messiness of reality aside. "We do."

"And you speak such excellent Japanese."

"Me? Not at all. I'm afraid I still have a long way to go." I had learned to wave my hand in front of my face in the standard gesture of modest denial.

People were especially impressed when I got gestures right, even the smallest of them. She laughed. "You are a *chinju*."

"What's that?"

"A *chinju* is a rare and valuable creature, the sort that you find in a fairy tale."

I liked the idea of myself as a *chinju*, maybe because the word felt archaic, rare and valuable in its own right. But I didn't like the more common term that I heard all the time, *henna gaijin*, which meant "strange foreigner," the kind of foreigner who showed excessive zeal in adopting Japanese ways. Foreigners were not supposed to do that. It was important that they remain foreign, a marker by which Japanese could define their Japaneseness. It was important that foreigners remain perennially lost, bumbling oafs who spoke too loudly and laughed without covering their mouths and failed to use chopsticks or take their shoes off at the door. And Japan, with its lack of street signs and its weird, non-geographic system of assigning house numbers, seemed to secretly collude in making them that way.

For this reason, a foreigner speaking Japanese in Japan was interesting to Japanese people as a sort of category confusion, an exception that proved the rule. There was, back then, a small number of Japanese-speaking Westerners who made a living appearing on TV game shows and variety programs; their one real talent seemed to be speaking Japanese while having blond hair. They would have to answer questions about various aspects of Japanese life, while expressing their surprise and admiration. Viewers loved this.

There was an idea that the language was too difficult for foreigners to learn, not only because of its complex grammar and the intricate cultural ideas about social status and politeness embedded inside it, but because it partook of the Japanese essence, which could not be understood by non-Japanese. You had to be Japanese to speak Japanese.

Deep down I agreed with that proposition: my desire to speak Japanese had already begun to blur with the wish to *be* Japanese. That wish was secretive and a little ashamed, because it was obviously pathetic and silly, on top of being deeply disloyal to my own origins. But I didn't want to be a foreigner anymore, an *outside person.* I wanted to be an inside person, a part of this mysterious group of people who knew where the subways went and what tunnel to take to get to the exit and what the signs said and what honorific particle to append to a sentence when speaking to an elder—people who had friends and never felt lonely.

Foreigners who spoke Japanese made many Japanese people nervous: language was open and permeable in a way that race wasn't, an unguarded border. People sometimes had a bad reaction, as when I asked an older woman on the train platform whether this was the train to Tokyo Station. She looked at me, scanned my face, her eyes went wide, her mouth dropped open, and she started to back up, waving her hands ... Or the time I called the house of a schoolmate and her mother put down the receiver and yelled, "It's the *gaijin* ..." or the Japanese mother-in-law of a British classmate who said to me, *Gaijin* can't speak Japanese.

Why not? I asked. It was a reasonable question since we were *speaking* in Japanese. Her daughter-in-law also spoke to her exclusively in Japanese.

"Because they can't understand the Japanese *kokoro*," she replied. "Only a Japanese can." *Kokoro* means "heart."

That assumption was deeply ingrained. I would speak to someone in

Japanese and they would address their answer not to me but to the Japanese person standing next to me, as if that person had somehow put the words into my mouth. I would listen and respond, and they would answer the other guy, making eye contact, smiling, and bowing while ignoring me—whole conversations went that way. Yet I still tried. I practiced bowing in front of a mirror. I practiced hand gestures. Before sleep, I reviewed my vocabulary cards, wondering if I would finally dream in Japanese. But my dreams were always in English—worse, they were always in New York, full of the ache of longing for the home I had fled.

Finally, near the end of my year, as the date for returning to the U.S. approached, I had coffee with a coed so many steps removed from the original coed that they didn't know each other, didn't go to the same school, had no friends in common. There was a different feeling to this coed, too, a different atmosphere. At a time when Japanese women tended to wear highly gendered clothing, shirts with bows and flounces, skirts with pantyhose, lots of pink, she was in jeans and a brown sweater, no makeup. She brought something with her to the coffee shop to show me, I forget what, a book, perhaps, as if our meeting were something serious, a school assignment.

We met a number of times after that in coffee shops. She never suggested a trip to a tourist sight; she didn't seem to be thinking of herself as somebody hosting a foreign guest. Finally, she made dinner for me at her place. I believe it may well have been the first time I'd been to a Japanese woman's apartment, *any* woman's apartment, and I felt as if I was seeing something mysterious and important, a glance into how I might be able to live, too. There was her bookshelf, with paperback translations of French and American writers. It led to an extremely inexpert kiss—almost a lunge—that seemed to shock her but not surprise her. The look in her eyes said that she had thought of this, too.

But we were out of time. I returned to New York and in September went back to college to finish my last year. I learned about my father's legal troubles, the secret that my family had kept from me for a full year, that had nevertheless oppressed me as silence.

She and I wrote back and forth. I have those letters in the box, too, but no intention of looking at them. It's not that they were empty, but rather, that they were over-full, and there was something about their fullness that made me feel dishonest and guilty, though I didn't even know how to begin thinking about the problem. Looking back, I just wasn't used to having feelings that needed describing. For the most part, I avoided saying what I felt. When I wrote to her, I felt the slippage of the written word, as I tried to find a convincing voice on the page—a voice that would convince her and feel genuine to me, too, but wouldn't have any of the pain or embarrassment of actual truth—that wouldn't do damage to either one of us. I never once mentioned my family's crisis. But I felt false for other reasons, too. How did I really feel about her? The truth was that I hardly knew her, and I barely had the mental space to include her. I was in a sort of deep mourning for the person I'd thought I was, the family I thought I came from, and from that vantage point the whole world seemed unknowable. Was I writing to her because I missed her or because she was my link to Japan? There were times when I wrote to her thinking that she would pull me back somehow, rescue me. And there were other times when she seemed like an annoyance, irrelevant, because I would clearly never get to go back. The situation with my father was so bad, I couldn't imagine the kind of personal liberation that Japan still represented to me, the dream of becoming some sort of new, free person. I would never learn to dream in Japanese.

I graduated from college, found a job at a publishing house, answering the boss's phone, and then a couple of months later, got a scholarship from the Japanese Ministry of Education to study at Tokyo University. It was unexpected: I was a second alternate. When I got the news, I quit my job, and within a couple of months, I was back in Japan, back in Tokyo, living in her neighborhood in an apartment she had found for me. Was I glad to be free of the troubles back home? Most definitely, but guilty, too, and I felt hobbled by the image of my father stretched out on the couch and staring at the ceiling, fat and unshaven, bleary-eyed from depressive insomnia. How could I leave them now in order to become Japanese? It seemed like the lowest form of betrayal.

She got angry with me often. I wasn't attentive enough. Or I was too attentive. Why couldn't I leave her alone sometimes? Why was I crowding her? I think she was conflicted about me. That shocked me; I considered myself so loveable, so fun, and so interesting. But she explained that she had grown up with the assumption that she would have to get married, that it was her job to find a husband while still in her mid-twenties, and that that husband would be Japanese, of course. She couldn't waste time on a *gaijin*.

There's a saying, she told me once. A girl is like a Christmas cake—it's half price after twenty-five.

That's terrible, I said, full of indignation on her behalf.

She didn't want to get married, she told me; she wanted to work and pursue a career. But most companies didn't want women hanging on in the office after a certain age. And her parents—her parents would be so disappointed.

Looking back, I imagine she believed that if there was no way out of getting married, then she should marry me. I was the most un-Japanese man she could possibly marry. I would allow her to continue working and have a career. The only problem was that she didn't *want* to marry me: she wanted to marry a real Japanese man, someone like her father, someone her parents would understand and respect. Someone *she* could respect. And so my presence forced the issue in a really irritating way. In effect, I created the whole problem; it was my fault. It would be so much better if I simply weren't around. And yet she didn't want to break up with me, either. It wasn't clear what the solution was.

All this charged and complicated talk about the meaning and direction of our relationship was terrifically upsetting to me. It wasn't clear to me who wanted to marry whom, or who wanted to avoid marrying whom. It changed from day to day: sometimes me, sometimes her. In any case, all I needed was to hear the English word *marriage* and I would feel an electric charge zap my nervous system, stop my breath, scramble my brain. My consciousness would go white like a TV with a busted tube. The associations were with my parents' marriage, which I considered, on one level, a priori perfect, since I loved them and considered them perfect in their complete imperfection, like mountains or great storms or wonderful chaotic cities (think Rome, think Taipei). On another level, however, what I had seen of marriage seemed like a continual miscommunication, two people arguing in two mutually unintelligible languages, shouting those mutually incomprehensible words across great chasms and through locked doors: anguished and lonely.

The Japanese word for marriage, *kekkon*, affected me differently, however. In Japan, at least back then, everyone got married. Single wasn't an option. *Kekkon* was woven into the texture of things; it was soothing, it meant you belonged, you had a family, roots, a place to go home to at the end of the day, not like my miniature apartment, with its little stack of books and its single table and its silence. You weren't lost, and you weren't a *gaijin*. You weren't alone.

At night, I went to sleep next to her, assuming that I would finally dream in Japanese. But my dreams were in English, even when she was in them, though we never spoke English together.

We didn't argue about marriage or *kekkon*; we argued about everything else. "Do you understand?" she asked me once. We were back to that first word from the first day of my first Japanese class: *Wakarimashitaka*?

"I do understand, but I don't agree."

Her eyes narrowed; she looked at me as if I were a simpleton. "That makes no sense. If you understand, you must agree."

"I definitely do understand. But I *don't* agree." *Wakattakedo, sansei dekinai.* I was saying that I could see her point of view, but felt her to be mistaken—that I had a different point of view. And yet even to my foreign ears it didn't quite sound right, as if I were combining two things that shouldn't go together.

"Then you don't really understand," she said, as if correcting a grammatical mistake. "In Japanese, understand *means* agree."

"But I don't agree."

"Then you don't understand."

"But I *do* understand. I see exactly how you feel. I just think you're wrong."

We went round and round, stuck at a cultural impasse and also a battle of wills. The two of us surprised, increasingly stressed, by this ridiculous linguistic problem, but unable to find our way out. It would have been easy enough to simply say, Fine, I *don't* understand, but I wouldn't do it. I prided myself on understanding, on empathizing. That was my unique skill as . . . whatever I was, an American observing the Japanese around him like a pickpocket looking for an easy mark. An actor studying for a role. A shape-shifting *chinju* ready to steal a new form. A dutiful son who imagined himself (it was always an illusion, probably) taking care of troubled parents, so that, in turn, they could continue taking care of him.

We solved it in the best worst way possible: I helped her get into graduate school in the United States. With a graduate degree she could have a real career in her field, perhaps even work in the U.S. instead of Japan; there would be more opportunity for a woman in the U.S. In a hallmark move, I arranged for her to stay with my parents, whom she came to loathe in a way that felt, well, a little ungenerous—their lives were unraveling, after all. Had I thought she might do something to shore them up? It's possible. The way she saw them, the accuracy of her lampoon of them in her letters, hurt me deeply, though I didn't defend them. In time she moved out and we dissolved. Maybe that was the intention all along—to find a way out that didn't require my saying that I simply wasn't ready yet.

But that was still in the future. I remember the day I saw her off: after she was gone, I walked to the subway, feeling as if the city would swallow me up, that it would pull me under as the sea pulls down a tired swimmer. I had so much time now and didn't know how to fill it. I started spending hours in the library, reading books in English, just for the soothing familiarity, the reminder of the safety of home, and because I found it too depressing to finish things, I wanted them to be long. That's how I alighted on Spenser's *The Faerie Queene*. Over the weeks and months, little by little, I read it to the end, feeling as if each of those arcane stanzas with their antiquated English and complicated rhyme scheme were a sort of crossword puzzle containing the answer to my loneliness.

I can't quite remember exactly how I met Mr. Tanaka, though I know it was through a friend—that chain of acquaintance once again.

Mr. Tanaka was a Buddhist priest. He was in his thirties, probably, and he dressed in ordinary street clothes; there was nothing obviously priestly about him, other than his shaved head. Though I kept expecting him to say something philosophical and priestly, it never came.

We were taking a little walking tour of his neighborhood, which was in Shitamachi, the oldest part of Tokyo, full of little shops and narrow alleys dotted with flashes of great beauty—a red arch the color of lipstick, a flight of stone steps leading somewhere shaded and mysterious. It was the kind of place I could see making my own and never leaving, forgetting the rest of the world even existed—the kind of place that made me hungry to belong.

We ended up at his temple, a squat, muscular structure with a swooping tile roof and massive pillars, squeezed between two modern buildings maybe four stories tall. We stopped at the incense holder and lit sticks of incense and waved the smoke onto ourselves. The interior was impressively dark, a marvelous Buddha statue sitting inside, glinting brass: Kannon, the goddess of compassion. But what I remember best is Mr. Tanaka's wife in a white apron standing on the gray granite steps in front of the temple after we stepped outside again. She had a gentle smile on her face that made me ache.

Those inchoate feelings. I realize now that I wanted the Tanakas' temple to be *my* temple, my *home*, that I wanted to live there with them. But they had children already—a little boy had come out to stare at me, wide-eyed.

Mr. Tanaka walked me back to the train station. My mood became wistful. I hated to go home. And as with many acquaintances, I wasn't sure when or if I would ever see him again. "Thank you for the tour," I said to him, bowing.

"I'm wondering," he said, and then asked if I'd be interested in teaching English conversation to a group of priests to which he belonged.

I hesitated. English conversation was a big thing in Japan: people paid huge fees just to talk to a native speaker for an hour, to sit next to their foreignness, their bulk and hairy hands, listening to the strange syllables of English floating through the air. But I avoided English—other than

The Faerie Queene—and I avoided foreigners and anything that foreigners typically did. The idea that I might be considered a typical foreigner filled me with dread. I'd been tempted into teaching English conversation only once, at an engineering firm, but my classes contained so little actual English, and so much instruction in Japanese, that I was summarily fired.

But I thought of the low dark temple and the Kannon glowing in the dark. I thought of Mrs. Tanaka and her smile. I said yes. And it turned out that Mr. Tanaka's group was perfect for me: the less English we spoke, the more we joked around in Japanese, the more they liked me. They looked relieved that nothing foreign would be required of them. We all went out drinking after class, and though I had feared that I would end up being treated as an on-call English-conversation resource, a professional foreigner, English was instantly forgotten.

Maybe *that* was the priestly thing about them, the way they included me effortlessly, without any self-consciousness. But I never lost the odd sense that I wanted something from them. That I wanted them to do something for me, or tell me something that I needed to know.

I saw Mr. Tanaka as much as possible, taking advantage of his good nature. I remember he once took me to a temple, and the temple grounds were full of tiny Buddha statuettes made of stone, some of them worn, stippled with lichen, others clearly new. These were Jizo images: Jizo is the guardian of children and travelers. You see them by bridges and on the side of the road wherever there's been a traffic accident. Through some kind of deep sympathetic transformation, they look a bit like babies themselves: bald head, round face, mysteriously calm expression. Some were dressed in bibs and smocks like babies wear; others had offerings of plastic toys, particularly pinwheels. Imagine an ancient temple yard, full of row upon row of baby-like figurines, a pinwheel planted before each one, spinning in the breeze.

"You are familiar with the story of Jizo?" asked Mr. Tanaka.

The rows of statuettes seemed like the loneliest sight in the world, the wish for rescue. They made me think of my brother and sister and my parents, their lostness. Of course, I was really thinking of my own. I felt an embarrassing rush of emotion and became terrified that I might suddenly begin to weep, that I wouldn't be able to stop myself.

"Yes, of course," I said, trying to keep it as light as possible. "As a traveler, Jizo-sama is my guardian Buddha."

"Yes, that's right," said Mr. Tanaka, glancing at me and then looking away. "Robaato-san, the other guys and I have been wondering if you'd be interested in joining us one evening to play *Tōsenkyō*. We could really use you."

I never told Mr. Tanaka or any of the others about my family. Instead, I learned how to play *Tōsenkyō*, a curious Edo-period drinking game, supposedly much loved in the pleasure quarters, in which you sail a fan across the room as if it were a paper airplane. The aim is to knock a target about the size of a saltshaker, called the "butterfly," off the box on which it stands. The butterfly is made of cloth; it is stuffed and brightly colored and looks something like a miniature jester's hat, with little bells hanging from either curved end. Scoring is arcane and wonderfully arbitrary, since it is based on nothing but how the butterfly falls relative to the fan and the box—each possible configuration named after a chapter from *The Tale of Genji*, the eleventh-century aristocratic tale of loss and erotic longing. Miss the butterfly completely, which scores nothing, and it is called "Calligraphy Practice," after chapter fifty-three, when the heroine Ukifune enters a nunnery to escape her jealous lover, Kaoru. Knock the butterfly off, but in a way that lands butterfly and fan on the ground separately, and it is worth just a single point: "Village of the Falling Leaves," after chapter eleven, in which Prince Genji has a brief affair with a woman of low rank. But all sorts of artful and surprising havoc is possible: the butterfly landing on the tatami standing upright (chapter forty-eight, "Young Sprout," ten points); the butterfly hanging from the edge of the box, failing to fall (chapter three, "Cicada Shells," eighteen points). Most improbable of all is probably "The Floating Bridge of Dreams," in which the butterfly lands upright on the tatami and the fan comes to rest on top of the butterfly but on top of the box, too, creating a sort of bridge. It references the last chapter of *Genji*, in which Kaoru finds Ukifune's nunnery. He spies on her there, but that's where the novel ends, in that suspended moment between obsession and the possibility of release. We don't know what he's going to do.

I was pretty deft with the fan. We put together a team and joined a sort of local league, something like a bowling league, made up of all sorts of people from Shitamachi, not just priests—I remember there was an insurance agent with deadly aim on one of the opposing teams that had us a little cowed. The key, I found, was to get into a sort of Zen state and just let the fan go while staring hard at the butterfly, forgetting everything else. At that moment, you are not yourself; you are not a *gaijin*, not a *chinju*. You are not speaking but you are not silent, either, because you are not thinking. There are no words in your head in Japanese or English. You are just sending the fan on its way through the air. All you have to do is let go.

Mono No Aware

I FIND IT BY accident, pressed between two large volumes on the shelf. Though it has been over twenty-five years, I recognize it instantly: a mere sliver of a book, about half the size of an American trade paperback, with tan card-stock covers smudged from handling.

This is my copy of *Yukiguni*—in English, *Snow Country*—by Yasunari Kawabata, the first novel I ever read from start to finish in Japanese. I hold it up to my nose, breathe in the musty smell, and feel a terrible mourning for the loony stupidity of my youth. The feeling is so strong and so complicated, so full of what the Japanese call *mono no aware*, the sadness of things, that I can only stand there with the thin little volume in my hands, half-wishing I hadn't found it, half-wanting to put it back.

Over the years, I'd come to think of myself as a failed student of Japanese: too soon frustrated, too easily distracted. But turning the pages of *Snow Country*, I am startled by the sheer amount of work I put into reading it. Notes are scrawled everywhere, in a childlike Japanese handwriting, and they contain almost no English. Rather than use a Japanese-English dictionary to look up the words I didn't know, I'd limited myself to a regular Japanese dictionary and obtained the definitions in Japanese, which meant that here and there I was forced to branch off and define a word in the definition, too—again, without resorting to English. It was a purist's semi-delusional procedure.

But then consider that I marked up my copy of *Snow Country* in a suburb of Tokyo, while living in a little six-mat room smelling sweetly of new tatami. I was a nineteen-year-old Japanese lit major who had never been so far from home, and I was both terrified and elated—the terror and elation sometimes hard to tell apart or disentangle, because I was also in love with everything around me: the local shrine with its stone steps and red gate, the trains clacking past, the smell of roasting chestnuts in autumn, the silvery drill of the cicadas at night. Of course, I fell in love with every woman I met, including my landlady, a widow in her sixties who would invite me in to eat red bean cakes and watch the sumo matches on her black-and-white TV.

I channeled all that desire and sense of being lost into learning Japanese, as if it were possible to slip into another life through another language. My notes focus only on grammar and vocabulary, the literal meaning of each sentence, but they seem to ache with an unspoken yearning. I didn't simply want to understand the book: I wanted to be a part of the culture that had produced it, wanted to dream its collective dreams and share its secret codes—wanted to belong.

I probably don't have to point out the absurdity of this wish. Japan was a pretty insular place back then, ambivalent about the outside world and uncertain about foreigners. Little kids would run from me on the street or, conversely, ask to touch my skin. There was no possibility of forgetting who I was, that I already had a history, a personality, a language, a culture, a family of my own.

But then again, don't we ask for doomed and hopeless things from books all the time? Looking at my notes, I feel that incredible emotional hunger come back to me, and I realize that Japan showed me what books are truly for: they are laboratories for our desires.

UNRELIABLE TOUR GUIDE

As a student in Tokyo in the 1980s I would often go to the local Shinto shrine just to listen to the quiet. The shrine was small and undistinguished, a gap between concrete commercial buildings reached by an alleyway lined with red *torii*, or ritual gates. Off to one side was a structure no bigger than a phone booth, all steeply pitched roof and closed doors, bound by a heavy length of sacred rope: the place where the spirit, the *kami*, lived.

I believed I could feel the presence of the *kami* in the narrow alley and weird little space between buildings, and in the sudden inexplicable quiet amid the noise of the city. It was the same sense of mystery I felt everywhere in Japan, just a little clearer, a little easier to locate. And so it was while standing there, at the shrine, that I decided I was going to write a novel as soon as I got back to America, because novels are shrines too, sacred spaces where you can feel the presence of things too deep to name.

Back in New York City a year later, I bought a typewriter and got ready to write that novel. The problem was that I also needed a job. At the age of twenty-three, my work experience was limited to teaching English conversation to a group of Buddhist priests in the Shitamachi, an older area of Tokyo. They had quickly introduced me to an Edo-period drinking game called *Tōsenkyō*, in which players try to knock down a little target by sailing an outspread fan across the room, much as if it were a paper airplane.

So when I sat down to consider my marketable skills, I identified just three: I was good at trading raunchy jokes with drunken clergy; I knew how to make an open fan swoop and glide across a room; and I could speak Japanese.

And then one day I was walking downtown, avoiding the novel I didn't know how to start, when I saw a tight formation of camera-toting Japanese in front of the World Trade Center, led by a woman carrying a little red flag. I watched them climb single file into a gigantic bus and lumber off.

Tour guide. I could be a tour guide.

What could be easier than walking around with a little flag, showing people the sights? It would require no commitment, no thought, and would leave my mind free for the novel that was even then, I believed, forming in my unconscious.

I called up one of the bigger companies and got an interview for the very next day. The man who would become my boss interviewed me standing up in a hallway, too busy to sit down. He was cadaverously thin, with big dark circles around his eyes—haunted-looking, as if the thought of losing a busload of tourists in the Bronx, clicking away at their cameras, made it impossible to sleep at night.

"Tell me," he asked in Japanese, "what do you think makes a successful tour guide?"

I hadn't given it a thought. "Well, my Japanese, while miserable and painful to listen to, is not completely impossible to understand," I said, all of which was a very Japanese way of implying that since my command of the language was good enough for Tokyo University, it would be good enough for a busload of rice farmers from Niigata on their first trip abroad.

"No, that's not it," he said. "It's not just the ability to communicate. A good tour guide is someone who wants to make people happy." He looked at me with great hopeful earnestness. "Do you like making people happy, Robaato-san?"

"Of course I do," I said, trying to smile like someone who might actually feel that way.

He didn't seem completely convinced, but a couple of days later I was at JFK, holding up the sign he'd handed me.

And then the doors slid open and they began to walk toward me, blinking uncertainly: a line of elderly Japanese in golf hats, thick glasses, and crepe-soled shoes. As they drew close, I could see them glance from my sign to my face, then look past me for someone else, the real tour guide.

In Japan back then, this kind of invisibility was the foreigner's constant dilemma, so it was a situation I understood well. I bowed extra low. "*O-tsukare ni narimashita*," I said: This has been tiring for you.

"You speak Japanese," said one. "What a relief."

"But you're not Japanese, are you?" said another.

While living in Tokyo, I'd gotten used to people simply not believing that I could speak the language, even as I was speaking it to them. They would look from me to the Japanese person standing next to me, assuming that the words were coming from that other person's mouth through some act of ventriloquism. What I felt was not sorrow or anger but a sort of tenderness. "Please accept my deepest apologies for not being Japanese," I said, bowing again. "It's true that I'm only an American, but I will nevertheless try my best."

Those closest to me bowed in return. Someone said, "I'm sure you'll do fine."

I got the group onto the bus and took it straight from JFK into a city tour that is a little blurry all these years later: Rockefeller Center, St. Patrick's Cathedral, Chinatown, Battery Park, Wall Street—they were all in there. I rode up front, the microphone in my hand. The guide I'd shadowed the day before on my one-and-only training run had kept up a steady stream of patter about the size, height, and cost of just about everything we'd passed, but somehow I hadn't thought to prepare anything of my own. Wasn't I born here? Hadn't I lived most of my life here? I'd just assumed that I could wing it, but as we rumbled on, I became aware that my pauses were getting longer and longer, the tourists watching me with concern.

So I began making stuff up.

Passing the Central Park Zoo, I mentioned the escaped tiger they were still trying to capture—how the park was safe during the day when it slept in its hiding place, but dangerous at night when it hunted. "You must absolutely stay out of the park at night," I told them.

"What does it eat then?" somebody asked.

"The rat problem is much better now."

Turning the corner on Seventy-Second Street, I noted the big brown bulk of the Dakota House. "To our right you see the place where internationally famed musician John Lennon was killed by a crazed fan. See that dark spot there? That's his blood. It's been left there as a tribute. The city doesn't wash this sidewalk anymore."

"I don't see any dark spot," somebody said.

"By the entrance. You have to look closely." Mercifully, traffic was moving pretty briskly. "The Dakota House is, by the way, the most expensive apartment building in the world, with apartments selling for tens of millions of dollars. The biggest spans the entire top floor and costs one hundred million dollars. The master bathroom is made of solid gold."

"Solid gold? Can't be."

"But it is."

Apparently nobody complained about my loose hold on the facts, because my boss began giving me customized assignments. I took two slightly raffish executives of the Japan Motorboat Racing Association up and down the East Coast on a tour of racetracks and casinos. I went to a series of fashion events with the Pearl Princess, who as winner of the Pearl Princess Beauty Pageant and official face of the Japanese pearl industry was required to wear a ceremonial kimono and a big pearl tiara at all appearances, though clearly hating every minute of it. I rode around town in the back of a stretch limo with a famous calligrapher who was something like the Keith Richards of the art form, in black turtleneck and sunglasses (I still have the piece he made for me). I spent two weeks at a golf resort in Florida with a rich elderly couple, serving as interpreter, caddy, and surrogate son, dressed up in the golf clothes they picked out for me in the pro shop.

There was something fascinating about the sudden false intimacy of those connections, spending all day with a stranger in airports and hotels, taking his or her smallest, most fragile wishes and translating them into a language he or she could not understand ("He says he wants starch on the front of the shirt, but not on the back . . ."). Often, it made me feel like Sancho Panza, humoring the madness of Don Quixote, but it also made me feel useful and therefore a little less existentially lost. And then too, there was an almost abstract quality of loneliness to the enterprise, because once the trip was finished and there was nothing left to translate, the people disappeared.

But I think the real reason that I continued as long as I did (three years, incredibly) was that it allowed me to speak Japanese all day. Wrapping myself in those long, intricate sentences, so different from anything possible in English, let me feel as if I hadn't ever really left Japan and therefore didn't need to begin figuring out the next phase of my life. It didn't matter that writing fiction was a lot harder than I'd ever thought, and that my novel was getting nowhere. Working as a tour guide, time itself seemed to have stopped moving forward, and I was safe from the future and whatever it might require of me.

I don't know how long I would have continued in the job, left uninterrupted; most probably I would have pulled myself together at some point. As it happened, the end came with an interpreting assignment for a guy representing his village's pearl cooperative; he had come to negotiate a deal with an American wholesaler located in the Diamond District, and so we took a cab from his hotel to that neighborhood full of Hasidic men in black hats and long beards, carrying little paper bags full of precious gems. The firm we visited was Hasidic, too, the owner a distinguished rabbi who sat behind a big desk in a room filled with heavy leather books in Hebrew.

"You're Jewish, aren't you?" he asked me.

"Yes," I said, feeling some trepidation. All the care and study in my life had gone into learning Japanese; I couldn't pass an impromptu Hebrew test, had never opened a volume of Talmud.

"Do you think they're going to help you when you're in trouble?" he asked.

"Who's they?" But of course I already understood. He had constructed a quick little story around me, in which I was trying to hide or deny my true identity—trying to get myself adopted by the Japanese as a sort of mascot. It was ridiculous, but it also hit home. My hands began shaking.

"I don't need any help," I said, barely squeezing the words out.

It was just a moment. He looked at me and frowned; we all went back to our discussion of pearls. At the end of the day I dropped my client off at his hotel, took the train home, and lay on my bed, replaying the exchange over and over again, excavating every layer of hurt.

The rabbi was both right and wrong, I knew. He was right in that I had a choice to make, but he was wrong in that the choice wasn't between the Japanese and the Jews. It was between then and now, and between now and the future, and between safety and risk, and between translating other people's desires and describing the world as I saw it, an enterprise by its very nature saturated with desire. It was between being a tour guide and telling the true story of the city I kept glimpsing out of the tour bus window: the story of the world I grew up in.

I got out of bed, went to the window, and pulled open the curtains. Darkness had fallen, and the quiet street in Brooklyn where I lived was almost empty. Someone was walking a dog, someone else carrying home groceries. Someone on Rollerblades sped toward Prospect Park.

Shopping

"MAYBE A NEW WRIST watch," my father said. "A gold model with diamonds around the face. And I know just where to go." He combed his hair with his fingers and put on a pair of aviators with yellow lenses, his antidepression glasses. "It's okay because we're not *really* buying. We're just making them *think* we're buying."

The store was hushed and intimate and very expensive looking: we had to be buzzed in from the street, and we were the only customers. But my father changed as we walked inside, just as he did when he walked into criminal court. He was a character now, an ever-so-slightly better version of himself, richer and more important—*merry*. As we looked at the watches, he talked.

"I know I shouldn't care about *things*," he said, turning the watch this way and that so the diamonds looked like bits of ice in the light. "But I grew up poor and I can't help it." We left only because we couldn't quite decide which model to get, the gold or the platinum.

Later, the salesman called us at home to tell us that a new and better watch had just come in, that he was holding it especially for us. Phone receiver to his ear, my father looked annoyed. "Listen, can you call me back in an hour?" he said. "I'm in the middle of something here." An hour later, we sat together and watched the phone ring till it stopped. But the salesman called again a few days later and I ended up telling him that my father couldn't come to the phone because he was sick with pneumonia. I thought that would be the end of it, but he called again a week or so later. "I'm sorry, my dad isn't here." He was in fact right there, listening, horrified and delighted, hanging on every word. "He's in the hospital."

After hanging up, I looked at my father and laughed. "Look what you made me do."

"This is terrible," he said, eyes wide with excitement. "I never meant for him to keep calling."

"Well, what do we do now?"

"Tell him I died. That will get rid of him."

HOMESTEADERS

My brother David wanted us to find an apartment together—me, him, and his two dogs, Bugsy and Roscoe, who had been in a fire and suffered from PTSD. We'd be a happy commune, without the sadness of parents. Everything our parents did in those days seemed to mourn the unexpected turn our lives had taken. If you glanced at my father at an unguarded moment he looked as if he were about to cry.

"Imagine coming home and nobody's yelling," said David.

Our mother did a lot of yelling. She was overwhelmed by her job as a lawyer for the city: the filing deadlines, the court dates, the judges who were petty dictators. She lived in fear of making a mistake. Plus, when she got home our father would be lying on the floor watching TV, a big bottle of antidepressants next to a bunch of dirty dishes. She would walk into the kitchen with her coat still on and start chopping onions. Nobody even thought of cleaning.

David and I did nothing to help out, either. It never occurred to any of us that we should. I think there was a depressive sense that nothing would make a difference—or that's how I rationalized it. All I could imagine was getting free.

"Imagine coming home and you can sit down on the couch," said David. The couch was covered in our mother's legal files. At night, in her nightgown, she would pick up one and then another, pacing up and down.

"We can't afford an apartment," I said.

"You can't stay here forever. It's not healthy."

Our parents' place was a four-bedroom duplex, but I had a feeling like I was in a tiny capsule and being crushed. There was a lot of aspirational junk shoved everywhere, because through some odd logic, the less money they had the more they wanted to buy things, though now they had to be cheap: an exercise device called a Bullworker that my father had bought off TV. Neckties he got at the thrift shop, a gigantic mound of them hung over a chair back. My mother had been buying a lot of things too: porcelain figurines and Buddha statues and old candelabras—things that didn't cost too much but allowed her to feel that she was still living a cultivated life.

Our parents had turned their bedroom into a home office for my father, now that he'd gotten his law license back and was trying to work as a lawyer again. They'd taken my bedroom, so I was camping in my sister's room—she was going to college. David was back in his old bedroom along with the two dogs.

"What about a nice two-bedroom downtown?" David said. He was working at a lab at NYU while applying to medical school. "That way I could walk to work."

I didn't believe such an apartment existed, not for what we could afford, around fifteen hundred bucks a month. But I went along with his project because it made me feel better just to sit and listen, half forgetting that it was all theater, a performance meant for the performers. I even agreed to go with him to a real estate agent in the village. When the agent there heard what we wanted and what we were able to pay he looked suddenly cautious, as if we'd come to pick a fight. "I don't think you'll find that," he said.

"Yes, we will," said David, suddenly furious, stalking out.

"That's the way they work," he said, marching home at double speed. "They tell you this is all you can get and you believe them and then they've got you. But I know there are good apartments out there. They're keeping them for themselves."

I don't know how he knew this, but he had an air of certainty. As a medical school applicant, he considered himself a man of science, a rational skeptic, a believer in evidence rather than rumor or common wisdom.

His certainty remained unchanged even when we began reading the classifieds in the back of the newspaper. Any apartment listing we could afford was way out in the boroughs, in a basement. David refused to go look at any of them, and when after many days of disappointment we finally went to see one, it was two rooms so small I found myself hunching my shoulders.

"Shit," I said. The place looked like two coffins laid side by side so the dead could talk through the wall.

"They lied to us," said David. "They said it was nice."

"Maybe this is what we can get."

"We're not living in a shithole like this," said David.

Back from that apartment, David and I sat at the dining room table, having an emergency meeting. We went over our list of preferences again—"I like a terrace," said David—which then somehow segued into plans for our futures.

"I've been reading about trauma surgery," said David. "Gunshot wounds, stabbings, car accidents. You're never bored." In a way, it was what our father used to do as a criminal defense lawyer: save people.

Mostly I listened and nodded. No matter how I tried, I couldn't think clearly about what my future might be like as a writer, maybe because I'd never written anything. Every time I tried to think about it, I'd start to get nervous and feel panicked and trapped and desperate. The beauty of being a tour guide was that the hours were so extreme that there was only the present, a space out of time.

Later that afternoon, our father came back from court looking surprisingly dapper in a suit and tie, his hair brushed back. He had good days, though it was unpredictable; on bad days he was in his underwear, letting his office phone roll to voicemail as he missed his court dates and watched TV and ate, methodically emptying the refrigerator. Only now do I really understand how hard it must have been, working in the same court building where he'd been sentenced to prison. All the court officers and law clerks and judges knew him from before.

He sat down and rubbed his face. "I hate criminals. They're all such fucking liars. This one today told me he was never there, but now they've got three witnesses." I listened, disturbed. It was such a change from the old days, when he loved criminals and watched them with distant amusement like a parent at the playground. Then he handed me a slip of paper with a name and number.

"What's this?" I asked.

"His name is Brian Covington. He's got an apartment for rent."

"But is it the right price?"

"I told him what you wanted to pay."

"But is it nice?" asked David. "For the money we're paying, we should get something nice."

"Call him and see." Our father seemed glad to be able to help—maybe he felt as if he'd let us down and wanted to make up for it. I don't know how he felt about us moving out. He never objected to us being there. Sometimes he seemed eager for company, late at night when he couldn't sleep. "Sit with me," he'd say, and we would sit there while he smoked, not talking but at least together. I remember watching his hand with the cigarette wavering, making the smoke squiggle. The lithium he took for his manic swings made his hands shake and it embarrassed him. He'd keep his hands in his pockets when he went to court.

"How's work?" he asked.

"Good."

"How are the Japanese?"

"Oh, the same."

He nodded and we sat in the silence until I couldn't stay awake and had to go to bed. But most of the time he seemed sealed off in his own world. Being around this version of him could feel very lonely.

An hour later David and I were walking into a huge new building on First Avenue, through a lobby with a two-story waterfall, up to the twenty-first floor in a golden elevator, and then into a big airy apartment. Light poured in through glass doors that led out to the terrace. It felt as if we'd left some kind of crazed, sick junk-shop storeroom for a palace: pristine, beautifully empty, and wonderfully expensive looking. We walked as if we might be ordered out.

It was Brian Covington who had that power, and we didn't know what to make of him. He was youngish, incredibly heavy—huge, actually—dressed in a skintight V-neck undershirt and gym shorts. He looked like a boy at summer camp blown up with an air pump till he was a parade float.

"Marble countertops," he said in the kitchen. "Wonderful light," he said in the living room. His voice sounded as if it were coming from someone else, a movie actress from the '30s. It was like getting an apartment tour from Vivien Leigh. "Come outside," he said, and pulled open one of the sliding doors to the terrace. The three of us lined up at the railing to look at the East River across the street: gray and muscular, liquid stone. The colored beads of cars slid down the FDR Drive.

I glanced at David, wondering what he made of this. He seemed giddy, his theories of real estate proved true at last.

"So what is it you gentlemen do, exactly?" asked Brian.

This was the interview segment. David explained his work situation and I explained mine, including the fact that I was trying to write a novel, something that I normally hid. I always felt foolish mentioning writing, as if it made me instantly transparent: suddenly everyone could see the ridiculous longing inside me.

And it was ridiculous, too, because I didn't write very much and had been on my first chapter for over a year. The novel was about my father and what had happened to him, to us, and writing it felt like a betrayal. We were doing our best to move forward, and we never mentioned the past. That made whatever I wrote seem sneaky and mean, a sort of revenge.

But I couldn't afford to be finicky now: I was trying to snag the apartment by being what my mother called *interesting.*

"Oh, you're a writer?" said Brian. "I'm a writer, too!"

David gave me an urgent look. I didn't like it when someone volunteered that he was a writer—I wanted everyone to be as conflicted as I was. But I asked the question. "Well, wonderful! What sort of writing do you do?"

"Oh, it's a memoir!" he said, sounding pleased to talk. "About running a brothel!" He gave a sigh and looked momentarily wistful. "I ran it out of this apartment, actually. Not *inside*, it was all outcall. But I would work the phones here with a couple of girls to help me out. I guess you could say that I was the madam."

"A brothel?" said David.

The wind from the river picked up, blowing our hair. The sun brightened. I felt a rush of excitement, and I could see that David felt it too: Brian was a criminal. We were in familiar territory.

"That's going to be a bestseller," I said.

"Well, I hope so," said Brian, looking pleased. "What I want to tell people is that it's a business like any other. I have no time for moralizing hypocrites."

Our family was all great listeners, beginning with our father. I'd grown up watching him listen to his clients tell him their troubles. He would take them in with his enormous liquid brown eyes.

Brian wanted us to know how hard he'd worked. "My clients were paying a lot of money for perfect service and I made sure they got perfect service." He wanted to tell us how much he had sacrificed in order to succeed. "We were so busy that I couldn't leave the phone to go to the bathroom. I couldn't take a day off. We ordered in three meals a day and I ate while I was answering calls. Look how heavy I got."

"So what went wrong?" I asked.

"Well, let me just say that I had many very important and distinguished clients, some of whom were in government, some of whom were foreign diplomats. And what I learned is that the FBI watches people at those levels. The business is closed, but there are unexpected positives. At least now I have some time for myself. And I have a lot of new things going on, the book, and a possible movie deal. I'm writing a TV pilot."

"And you're okay with fifteen hundred a month for this apartment?" asked David.

"You know, I could get more, of course, but I love young people just starting out. It's such an exciting time of life."

Plus, he needed tenants who could work with him. He had rented this apartment and the one next to it on a long-term lease, planning to knock down the walls and combine them. He had made this clear to the management from the beginning, but the building had changed its mind at the last minute and tried to block him, so now he was suing. He lived in the other apartment, and he'd decided to sublet this one out till the case was finished; when he won, we'd have to go so he could start construction.

"How long will that be?" asked David.

"Their only strategy is delay."

David's dogs were no problem, he told us; he had a Yorkie—dogs were kinder and sweeter than humans, don't you think? He showed us the big multi-line phone system inside and told us we could use one of his lines, which would save us from having to deal with the phone company. All he asked is that we use the service entrance in the back of the building instead of the lobby. "If anyone asks, tell them you're my cousins and you're staying with me for a little while." He didn't want further complications with the management. We wrote him a check for the first month and he gave us a set of keys.

Going down in the elevator, David and I began bouncing up and down with excitement, and then he stopped and said, "I told you so."

"It's a weird situation, though."

"That's a good thing—he needs us."

It also helped explain the super-cheap price, which had been bothering me. It was obviously worth much more. "How much of that was bullshit, do you think?"

"All of it, maybe, or none of it. Who cares? All that matters is that we're in."

After dinner, we packed up David's old station wagon and brought everything over, lugging it through the back entrance, the doorman stationed there watching with wry interest as we loaded the service elevator. We told him we were Brian's cousins, and that seemed to amuse him even more. I shouldered a loose mattress; David carried another; we toted up garbage bags stuffed with clothes, and then led the two coughing, trembling dogs inside. Once in the apartment, the stuff we unpacked looked old and tattered and stained.

Our parents hadn't really remarked on our leaving. Our mother had papers spread over the dining room table; she had some kind of deadline the next day. My father had experienced some kind of setback in court; he looked visibly frightened, biting his lip, his eyes wide open and staring. He would not say what it was, just shook his head.

I didn't know if they were resentful, or if I just wanted them to be. Maybe I was the one who was resentful. I guess I wanted our moving out to matter, as if it were our big launch into the world, the first apartment experience.

"Now what?" I asked David, glancing around our new living room. It was night. The city lights looked beautiful and melancholy outside the windows.

Before he could answer, we heard Brian's voice. "Is that you? Are you there?"

We both looked around.

"The intercom on the wall," said Brian. "Press the button and speak."

There was indeed an intercom set into the wall, silver and black, though I hadn't noticed it before. I walked over and pressed the talk button. "Yes, we're here."

"This and the phones were the only thing I got done before they changed their mind. I'll be right over."

He let himself in with the key a minute later, without bothering to knock. He'd forgotten to explain the situation with the electricity, he said: he got the bill for both apartments, so when it came he'd tell us how much and we'd pay him. Sure, no problem, we said. But he seemed reluctant to leave, and soon he was entertaining us with more stories about his career as a madam, this time about the people who used to work for him. "My fucked-up children, the family I never had."

"I've always wondered who goes into that kind of work," said David.

"Anyone who needs a lot of money fast. You could do it."

"No, thanks, I've already got a job."

"How much did they make?" I asked.

"A lot, though they always wasted it all and then needed more. I spoiled them rotten. I let them take complete advantage of me. And then, since I went to jail, not a word from any of them."

This took a beat, the jail part. It should have been obvious, but I hadn't thought of it before: I'd been totally focused on getting the apartment.

"Really, it was a kind of vacation," he continued. "They put me in the gay men's section, and we spent most of the time voguing." He started to catwalk across the living room in his T-shirt and gym shorts, massive but surprisingly nimble, stopping to strike poses out of an imaginary fashion magazine for very fat men.

This struck us as incredibly funny, and we howled with laughter. We were in our first apartment; it was super luxurious, and we were making friends with our landlord, who was weird and rich, a kooky character in the novel starring us. It felt as if we were in a convertible racing up Park Avenue at midnight with the top down, free.

Looking back, I can see that it was really sorrow that made us laugh so hard. When our father got back from prison, he would sit in the dark and cry. But he never talked about it. His time behind bars was a blank around which everything in our family revolved. But Brian was open about it, and funny. The lack of shame was exhilarating. "How long were you in for?" asked David.

Brian struck a pose, leaning on one hairy leg. "Not too long. Really it was just a problem with the bail arrangements. Once that got solved, I was out."

Later, after Brian had finally gone back to his apartment, our feelings started to shift. David and I stood out on the terrace, looking downtown, our parents' building somewhere among the lights. "Did you notice how he walked right in without knocking?" I asked.

"Yeah, I definitely noticed that."

"Shouldn't we talk to him about it?"

"I don't know. Maybe we should let it slide for now." We were getting a bargain, and we didn't have a lease, so we shouldn't risk offending him—we both saw that.

"He seems lonely," I said.

"That doesn't mean he can hang around all the time."

Back inside, I used the big multi-line phone to call home and got my father. "How's it going?" I asked.

"Okay," he said. The TV was on in the background, loud.

"So we're in the apartment," I said. I guess I wanted him to tell me that he missed us, but the TV just got louder; he would turn up the dial when he didn't want to talk.

"I'm in the middle of a program," he said.

"Okay, sure, maybe tomorrow."

"Yeah, tomorrow."

That night, I lay in bed, unable to sleep, feeling the strangeness of the new room. The place looked the opposite of a bordello—pristine white walls, blond wood floors—but it still felt wrong, and I wondered if Brian was lying and something had happened here. I thought I heard the front door opening. But when I padded out, the room was full of nothing but moonlight, glowing. I put the chain on the door.

Around this time, I got my father a day's work on a tour with me; it was a sign of how much he needed the money that he said yes—it was going to be around a hundred bucks for a very long day. I remember him in the hotel lobby in the early morning, dressed in a suit and tie that were way, way too good for the job, relics of his time as a successful lawyer. He was showered and shaved and his unruly hair was neatly brushed with pomade to keep it down. Something about the eager pains he'd gone through made me regret the whole idea—I didn't want to see that hopefulness. Maybe he was regretting it, too; he pulled me aside. He had an exquisitely fragile, emotional face, with huge brown eyes that seemed to quiver with the fear of humiliation. "Listen, I'm going use a pseudonym," he said.

"A false name?"

"Yes, call me Leo."

"Leo?" I don't think there was any meaning to the choice beyond the self-mocking tone.

"Like the lion. Don't call me Stanley."

"But I usually just call you Dad."

"Don't call me that, either. Use Leo."

I spent the day devising ways to not use a name at all, and then I slipped up in a moment of confusion—we were unloading suitcases in a hurry. "Hey, Dad, that one there."

One of the bus drivers snorted with laughter. My father was very fat and at moments like this one he looked like a baby inexplicably dressed like a flashy salesman. He froze, blinked, and then recovered with great dignity. "Yes, I've got it," he said, reaching for the bag.

All this make-believe was part of a wider pattern: we went to enormous lengths to cover up my father's legal troubles and his joblessness. My parents' friends and neighbors knew the truth, but they preserved a delicate silence, picking up on whatever story my father was telling that day and delicately adding to it as needed.

"I just couldn't stand retirement anymore," he told a friend of his who had come over for lunch.

"Of course not," the friend said, meditatively stirring his cup of tea.

"It was too quiet. So I'm back to practicing law," my father said, which was true, he'd just gotten his law license back after a hearing at which his psychiatrist had testified.

It was one of his really bad days. His face looked as if he'd attacked a mustard jar—not just his mouth but his cheeks and nose were pasted with mustard. There was a dot of mustard over one eyebrow.

"You'll get back in the swing of it," said the friend.

"Yeah," said my father, looking haunted. "I guess you don't really forget how to try a case."

"No, it's the proverbial bicycle."

I had a tendency to lie to the tourists, too. I couldn't help it: I would look out the window of the bus at the streets of Manhattan, the world I'd grown up in, and feel an odd sort of protectiveness, a desire to make it less sad for everyone. I lied about the price of X, and Y, and Z.

The lying felt necessary in the moment but made me feel guilty afterward. I worried that the tourists, so apparently eager to believe, suspected that I was in fact lying to them, and that one of them would tell my boss, Yoshii-san, who seemed to spend his entire life in the office, pouring over spreadsheets with flight times and hotel reservations and bus numbers, and making frantic phone calls. Whenever I stopped by, he would squint at me in a pained and long-suffering way and lecture me in Japanese about what I privately derided as the Way of the Tour Guide. I told myself that it was the same old bullshit I'd encountered in Japan, that Yoshii-san didn't trust me to do the job just because I wasn't Japanese. But secretly I wondered if he suspected the truth.

"Do they write to you when they get home, Robaato-san?" he asked me. "You know you have done a good job when they write to you thanking you for taking care of them."

"I get letters all the time," I lied.

He narrowed his eyes at me, as if trying to read my disloyal Caucasian face, and then the phone rang and he picked it up and began talking in a low murmur.

I left. I told myself that he was a corporate shill, that he didn't even believe all that nonsense, but actually I wished I would get one of those letters. I didn't like waiting on the tourists, getting them their dry cleaning at the hotel, and to salvage my dignity, I pretended to look down on them. That wasn't hard to do: it was the era of the Japanese tourist with his camera and his light meter; the people on my tours were gauche and unsophisticated, first-time travelers often more interested in confirming their prejudices than in letting the world flow in. But the truth was that I liked them, liked the little conversations at lunch in Chinatown or at the top of the World Trade Center observation deck, which were never about America, always about Japan, a world I transmogrified in my memory as safer and more certain than this one.

The thought of Yoshii-san looking at me with disappointment would keep me awake at night. The thought of being late to a hotel departure made my eyes shoot open and my heart race. I had nightmares about being fired. It wasn't just the money: I depended on my job to keep me from working on the novel, that terrible betrayal of my father containing all the truth we did not speak about.

But then suddenly the season began tapering off, and the travel office stopped calling. I had enough money saved up to last a while and just focus on the novel, so what I needed was to find new ways to fill the hours so I couldn't write. I paced the beautiful, empty apartment, a squeamish low-level panic churning inside me, like electric current circulating around and around. It was as if there were a thought I must not have, something sitting in plain sight that I must absolutely not look at—that kind of nervousness. I would stand on the terrace and watch the river flow. It was lonely, and I was extravagantly grateful when Brian called me on the phone to talk. He wanted to tell me about his memoir. I'd thought it was finished and sold and on its way to becoming a movie, but he still seemed to be working on it, thinking things out. He would run over his ideas with me, less like a writer and more like a salesman practicing his pitch.

"You pay for food, so why can't you pay for sex?" he said. "People need it, and they should be able to buy it."

"Sure," I said, though I could sense something fatally wrong with the idea.

"My clients were CEOs and movie stars. My agent wants me to name names, but it's against the madam's code. Then again, not a single one of these people came forward to help me when I got into trouble. So I guess I'll think about it."

"Why would a movie star need to pay for sex?" I asked.

"Because they want what they want when they want it. Same reason you go to a restaurant instead of cooking."

"Who are we talking about here?"

"I'm not saying."

Looking back, I don't think it's surprising that I somehow connected Brian and my father, that they blurred in my mind. They were both energetic rationalizers. Listening to Brian go on about prostitution wasn't all that different from listening to my father talk about the constitutionally mandated role of the criminal defense lawyer, who did not consider guilt or innocence. They were both fat, the sort of fat that whispered of compulsion and shame. Other people looked down on them, but I understood them as human beings with the same mixture of vulnerability and yearning that everyone contained. They had both gone to jail. They were both making new lives for themselves.

The difference was that my father was destroyed by what he went through—the shame, the sense of failure. It made me ache to see him in his present state, his hands shaking from lithium. But Brian seemed to have no taint of the past. He'd walked away from the wreckage and was on to the next thing. A part of me suspected that that was because Brian wasn't a good person—my father was a very good person, loving and kind. But I was angry with him for being weak in a way I wasn't angry with Brian.

I began to fantasize that Brian would help me in some way. Maybe his TV series would get taken and I could write for the show. Maybe he would introduce me to his agent. Maybe he would need some help with the movie. I knew a couple of people from college who had started careers with the help of a really good mentor. Maybe Brian would be my big break.

That night, there was a knock on the door. It was Brian, dressed up in khaki pants and a button-down shirt—the first time I'd ever seen him in anything other than the undershirt and gym shorts. "I'm going to Atlantic City," he said. The casino flew him to New Jersey by helicopter, he explained; the heliport was just across the street, by the river—one of the reasons he had chosen this building. He had only a few minutes to get over there if he was going to make his flight.

I'd seen those helicopters rising from the little fenced-in helipad, looking so incredibly important and urgent. In a few minutes Brian would be in one, sailing through the night sky.

"The beauty of being a high roller," he said.

He left, and I went out on the terrace watching for his helicopter. There were a succession of them landing and taking off into the patent-leather darkness, and I didn't know which was his.

One night Brian knocked and said he was going to Atlantic City by bus.

"No helicopter?"

"All booked up." He asked if I could walk his dog if it got late. He'd leave the door open so we wouldn't need a key. And then David got home and we did the obvious and walked down the hall to Brian's apartment just to take a look.

What we found was a weird mirror image of our own place: a single couch in the middle of the vast living room and a mattress on the floor of the bedroom, and virtually nothing else. The T-shirt and gym shorts were on the floor. There was an enormous walk-in closet, but almost nothing hanging in it. We went back to the living room and stood in the middle of all that nothing, his little dog running around our feet.

"It's creepier than finding a body," said David, looking around at the bare white walls.

Weirdly, it took tremendous mental effort to put the stunningly obvious pieces together. It was like trying to solve a logic problem on the SATs. "He's in Atlantic City trying to make money," I said.

"Everyone in a casino is doing that," said David. "That's why you go."

"No, I mean he *has* no money."

We retreated back to our own living room and flopped on the couch to think about this new idea. We'd both seen the casino buses waiting to take off outside of Grand Central and on Mott Street in Chinatown:

full of retirees, the elderly, they took three hours to reach Atlantic City and gave you forty dollars in chips to use at the casino. Somehow, that doomed us. "I don't want to go back to the parents," said David.

"We could rent a real apartment," I said.

"We can't afford one. Not one like this."

"Maybe we should talk to him."

"What good would that do?"

By now, Brian meant more to us than just the apartment, or perhaps it's more accurate to say that the apartment meant more to us than just a place to live: there was something about the space and the view and the luxury and the specialness that seemed to speak to our futures, our possibilities, whether the world would be kind or cruel. We overlooked the fact that we had no furniture, only a few cups and plates, that we came and went through the service entrance in back, where the Dumpsters full of garbage were kept. We talked in circles for the rest of the night—we were good at those circles—and then said nothing to Brian about what we had figured out.

He stopped by a couple of days later to collect the next month's rent, dressed in the undershirt and gym shorts.

"You boys are such a pleasure to have around," he said. "I like the company. I've come to think of you as the little brothers I never had." He offered us a deal: we could prepay the next month and he would give us a discount.

"How much?" asked David, looking shrewd.

"Oh, I don't know. Say, twenty percent?"

"You're on."

We did it again a couple of weeks later, when Brian dropped by to say that he found himself mysteriously low on cash. And then again a few weeks after that. We were now three months ahead on our rent. Then a few weeks later, we were four. "No more," I told David.

"Why not? He needs the money and it locks us in. Now he can't get rid of us."

"Why would he get rid of us?"

"This place is worth a lot more than we pay for it. He could always get somebody who would pay him more."

"But what if something goes wrong?"

"For an apartment like this, I'll take that chance."

It was then that the lights went out, and we lived in darkness for a couple of days. At first Brian told us that it was a mechanical failure, and only later that it was a billing problem. We had been paying him our share—so what had happened? A terrible, ridiculous accounting error. We passed over the question of where our payments had gone. He negotiated with the electric company brilliantly, working his way up to a vice president of some kind, until he arrived at a settlement, a great deal that would cost us only pennies on the dollar. But to lock in the bargain we'd have to pay the bill right away. Would we give him the money? If we did, he'd give us a free month's rent, which was worth a lot more.

The truth is that we had to say yes. We were already paid up four months in advance and couldn't live in the dark all that time. So now we had five months free living ahead of us, which was good because both our bank accounts were finally empty.

I stopped by my parents' apartment and found my father in his underwear, watching TV. "Hey, Dad," I said, "I'm worried about our situation with Brian Covington. Can you talk to him for us?"

"Me? I don't know if it would do any good." He stared at the TV.

"Where do you know him from?"

"I met him in an elevator in the criminal court building. I was telling someone how you were looking for an apartment and he said he had one."

"The criminal court building?"

My father didn't answer. He would often just choose to stop speaking, as if it were all too much bother.

It was a little later that Brian came to us with a letter from the building saying that it knew he was subletting to us, that it was in violation of his lease. He told us that, given the delicacy of the litigation already underway, we'd have to go.

"Well, give us back our money," said David.

"I will, definitely, but I'll need a little time."

"I want it now."

"If you act like a brat, I won't give it to you, ever."

David decided that we would get our money back or at least get revenge. Maybe there was something we could use to force him to pay us back. We went over to Brian's when he was out, found the door open, and did a search. What we found was a cardboard box containing papers, neatly sorted: court papers. The legal battle with the building was an eviction over nonpayment, not a disagreement over construction: Brian had *never* paid his rent, from the moment he moved in. It turned out that he wasn't finished with his other legal problems, either. He had been released from prison temporarily while the court decided an issue involving his medical treatment in jail. He had argued that he wasn't getting proper medical attention as a prisoner. This led us to medical reports: he was HIV positive. There were test results with numbers that David seemed to appreciate: "Not great," he said. "Pretty bad, actually." Brian was sick, though you couldn't see it. He was going to die, sooner rather than later. "Who knows how long he'll last," said David. And then finally we came on a letter addressed to the judge, asking for leniency. And it was from *another* judge, a judge in North Carolina, and he used a different name for Brian, *Morris—Morris Guller* was the full name—and he called him *My brother.* And he asked for mercy.

Before my father was sentenced, I had written a letter like this, asking for mercy. I'd fantasized about writing an angry letter, telling how he had been railroaded by overzealous prosecutors, how his livelihood had been destroyed over the course of an investigation that was more like a one-sided war of attrition, a carpet bombing. I wanted to write about how we had suffered. But I didn't write any of that. I wrote about what a good father he was and how much I loved him and would miss him if he had to go to prison. I wrote it in a sort of blank state, watching my hand move, as if I weren't a whole person but just a collection of limbs.

I did not understand mercy then. I was ashamed to ask for it. I was angered by my own desire to give it.

We put the papers back in the box, put the box back in the big near-empty closet, spent the next few hours getting our stuff into David's station wagon—using the service entrance—and drove back to my parents' apartment.

First Car

IT WAS A CADILLAC convertible from the mid-1960s, though I can't remember the exact year. It must have been twenty years old when I got behind the wheel—but it had been lovingly restored by its true owner, a client of my father's named Howie Shapiro, a former drug addict working his way through culinary school. It was white, with extraordinary fins in back and a big chromium grill in front. It was nearly a block long, or felt as if it were, and I could barely see over the dashboard, but the engine was perfectly silent, and the steering wheel moved with the touch of a finger. The mere thought of tapping the gas pedal sent the machine gliding forward like a great white shark. Did I mention that the interior was red leather? And the radio was incredibly loud? The thing was brash, devoid of self-doubt—all the things I wanted to be.

The car was Howie's, but he had nowhere safe to park it, so my father stored it for him in the garage under our apartment building. My father may have started out with good intentions; good intentions are a family trait. In this case that would have meant keeping the Caddy safe under the tarpaulin, probably, but pretty soon he was driving it around town, and then I was driving it, too, and then Howie seemed distracted by his own problems (money, sobriety, marriage, cheese soufflé). After a while, he stopped coming by to check on it, and I didn't see him again for a long time.

I took it on a camping trip, of all things, with a bunch of college friends. I didn't have a tent, so I planned to sleep in the car—the front seat was as big as a couch; I could completely stretch out on it, and a friend of mine took the back seat. But during the night I kept rolling into the horn, which was unbelievably loud, the brass section of some kind of gigantic dream orchestra. No one slept too well, even the squirrels. But I wouldn't leave the car. I had latched on to the idea of sleeping in it as some kind of self-conscious gesture of cool.

My sister, Perrin, was moving to Chicago to go to art school, and we drove her out there in the Caddy. A friend of hers by the name of Jan Chelminski did most of the driving—he would speed along at about a hundred miles per hour, with a single finger wrapped around the steering wheel. With the top down it felt as if we were flying at an altitude of about one foot over the payment, a very naked feeling, both frightening and magical. I remember falling asleep in the back seat out of sheer exhaustion—an incredibly deep sleep—and then waking up, unsure for the briefest moment where I was. The wind was beating at my head and the trees were rushing by, and beyond that there was nothing but fields. It was like waking up from a dream into a different dream.

Some years later, I was driving down the street in a car I actually owned, a Chevy Impala with a ripped-up interior that I'd inherited from my grandfather, when I recognized the Caddy up ahead—there was no mistaking that magnificent beast. The top was down and my father was behind the wheel, and next to him was a friend of his, Jim Kirk, who was dying of cancer. I knew that my father took Jim out on drives, but I'd heard it from my mother, not from him; I was living in Brooklyn at that point, and there was a bit of unacknowledged distance between my father and me . . . which is a way of saying that I don't know what ultimately happened to the Caddy. I ran into Howie some years after that on the street, but he looked like a junky again, wearing those mismatched clothes from Goodwill. He said hello and then darted away.

SEAN

THE FIRST TIME I saw Sean, I had no idea that we would become brothers. I watched him wander through my parents' living room, with its supply of child-lethal bric-a-brac, then gathered my courage and picked him up, just to be on the safe side. I was twenty-four and had no experience with toddlers. "See this?" I said, holding up a little brass Buddha. "This is a wise man with some kind of sharp pointy crown on, so be careful."

"Yes," said Sean, taking it in his hands. He was one and a half, not timid or shy, just limited to a small pool of words.

"And this is Hanuman, king of the monkeys."

"Yes," he said again, taking that statue, too.

Thirty years later, I recognize how fragile was the chain of circumstances that brought us together, how one slight alteration would have left us strangers. My mother worked for child welfare as an attorney prosecuting abuse and neglect cases; some months earlier, she had been assigned a case involving one of Sean's brothers, who had gone to the hospital with a broken arm of the kind that usually comes from parental yanking, and who had then gone back later with a third-degree burn from an iron. The four boys had been farmed out to different homes, and for the older three, those homes had become permanent. Only Sean was left. He suffered from persistent nightmares that forced him awake, screaming; a series of well-intentioned but sleep-deprived people had ultimately declined to take him on permanently. The one immediately before us had reached the end of her endurance and decided she needed a break—right away. Sean was with us, I was told, for just a few days, on an emergency basis.

To be honest, I can't remember how deeply his story penetrated my self-absorption. My big obsession back then was trying to figure out how to write a novel in the interstices of the kind of absurd part-time jobs (door-to-door furniture salesman, tour guide) that only the hapless recent college grad can stumble into. I had no particular sensitivity toward little kids and no desire for a new sibling. I already had two: David and Perrin were both away at college. We were exceptionally close, members of an exclusive club devoted to deciphering our eccentric parents and complex family history. We tended to be inward looking, wary of the outside world.

While Sean watched some cartoons on TV, I sat with my parents at the dining room table. "So you've got him for the weekend?" I asked, looking at the diaper bag, that strange, padded piece of luggage.

"The week, probably," said my mother.

"Could stretch longer," said my father.

A nervous silence. My parents looked exhausted already: two people in their middle fifties who had lived hard lives and were not in the best physical or emotional condition. My father reached for his bottle of antidepressants and swallowed one thoughtfully, as if in preparation for the challenges ahead. But beneath the air of quiet terror there was some other feeling, something steely and certain. They looked like gamblers who had stumbled on a not completely certain but nevertheless highly probable thing: the jackpot that might very well make their lives good again.

I was alarmed. My parents were decidedly high maintenance. Now that David and Perrin were away, I got all the calls for help: my mother needed a lift somewhere, needed me to wait in the apartment so a repairman could get in, needed me to convince my father not to do something disastrous (usually involving money). For his part, my father needed me to help him to the doctor when his back went out, or to file papers at court so he didn't miss a deadline—or just needed company when the melancholy of daily life became too much. Both of them wanted me to listen and untangle their many complicated and vociferous disputes with each other, involving spending, housecleaning, mistakes, and slights sometimes a quarter century old. I would drop everything and rush over to their place from my apartment in Brooklyn, an hour away.

The last few years had been especially hard on my father. Once a prominent criminal defense attorney, the sort you would see interviewed on the local news about some big case or other, he had been reduced to taking whatever floated his way. He now worked out of a tiny home office off the living room, with a desk covered in dirty laundry and fancy Italian shoes—he loved shoes—and a phone he never answered; he met with his clients in the McDonald's across the street.

All this worked in Sean's favor. Common sense, caution, a respect for order, solid finances, and a full night's sleep—all the things that had stopped previous families from adopting—were not my parents' concerns. What they wanted was love, the kind of love that would propel them through their midlife confusion. Sean came that weekend and never went back; my parents filed for adoption. They lasted through a year of his nightmares and frustration tantrums until the sheer constancy of their attention quieted the fear inside him. They took meticulous care of his asthma, and it, too, began to improve; there were fewer and fewer late-night trips to the emergency room. He started to talk more, and then it became a flood. The silent little boy was now a nonstop commentator on the world around him, smart, observant, and relentlessly opinionated. I started to notice phrases reminiscent of my parents: "Who knew?" he would say, an all-purpose exclamation of surprise and satisfaction whenever an unexpected treat came his way. "Who knew?"

My mother and father seemed to relish this second chance at parenthood. Always tottering on the edge of exhaustion, overloaded with plastic grocery bags, they nevertheless looked grounded, certain of their place in the world. I remember my father pushing Sean around the neighborhood in a stroller as if he were chauffeuring a celebrity. I remember my mother at home in her nightgown cradling Sean in her arms and cooing with deep satisfaction.

Of course, they couldn't stop being feckless, either—and, to be fair, their schedules were now so complex that even the most organized would have been overwhelmed. I still got the emergency calls, but instead of having to take care of my parents, I now had to take care of the little boy my parents were supposed to be taking care of. I complained, of course, sputtering over the phone about how important my time was, blaming them for preventing me from becoming a writer, but I never hung up on them. The truth was that the hours I spent with Sean were among the most genuine, human moments in a life that had become confusing and a little bit lonely. When I first took up fiction, I was under the impression that you composed a novel by pulling out a piece of paper and writing down whatever occurred to you, just as it popped into your head. But it didn't seem to work that way. After a couple of years of trying, the silence of the empty page had become frightening.

Taking care of Sean was something of a mystery too, but at least it felt alive. I had no idea how to entertain him at first, and my parents gave me no pointers. I took him to the park and experienced the strange slowdown of kid time, something I would relearn many years later after my own children were born: those long, lyrical moments in which you do somersaults on the grass or play excruciatingly cute games of peekaboo, only to check your watch and find that exactly two minutes have gone by, and the rest of the afternoon still stretches ahead.

Once, I cheated and took him to the movies, a grown-up movie, no less, as there were no kids' films playing nearby. It was safe enough—a romantic comedy with Tom Selleck, no violence, no sex—but looking back, I marvel at how I could have rationalized that move. Desperation, of course. I sank into the padded seat with utter relief, and the movie, at which I would normally have sneered, was bliss, simply because it did not involve pouring wet playground sand into a broken dump truck. I followed its every plot turn with such deep gratitude that I remember it all to this day. Sean was quiet enough for me to pretend that he might be content, though when I finally looked over I found him standing in his seat, facing the back of the theater, as if the show were supposed to materialize there. I realized then that he had never been to the movies before. "No, you watch the screen," I said, pointing. "The screen, over there."

"Why?" he asked.

"So you can see the movie." I watched him turn to dutifully stare at the giant image of Tom Selleck, and I saw the sad folly of what I was doing: his needs would have to come first because he was a little kid. It was that simple. "Come on," I said. "Let's get some candy. We'll go to the park."

Even as a rather callow twenty-four-year-old, still hanging on to a long list of adolescent grievances, I started to gain some grudging appreciation for my parents: if nothing else, they had staying power.

HAVE I MENTIONED THAT out in the larger world, Sean is considered black and the rest of us white? That we are brothers stuck on opposite sides of that strange classification system known as race?

Two and a half years after joining the family, when Sean was four, he seemed to realize for the first time that his skin was a different color from ours. I remember a confusing episode in a Chinese restaurant over the holidays, when Perrin and David were both back from college. It's possible that the sudden re-expansion of the family had left him feeling a little lost; in all probability, he wasn't getting much attention at dinner that night, sitting in a chair next to Perrin, his head barely above the table, as the adults yelled over each other in the crowded room and the dishes came and went. Suddenly, he blurted out, "Everyone has white skin except me!"

The conversation around the table stopped. "What did you say?" asked my mother.

"Everyone has white skin except me!"

The woman I was dating at the time was Japanese. "I don't have white skin," she said, holding out her arm. "See?"

"You're not *brown*," said Sean, sounding disgusted at this quibble.

"What's wrong with brown?" asked Perrin.

"I hate brown!" He didn't seem sad so much as frustrated and angry. His face quivered on the edge of tears.

We all began talking in a nervous rush, not so much to console him, I think, as to drown him out with our reassurances—reassurances meant for ourselves as well. "Brown is beautiful," said my mother. "Like chocolate."

"I wish *I* were brown," said my father.

"Brown is my favorite color," said David.

No one knew the magical words that would make this problem disappear, but then a moment later it was simply gone, as mysteriously as it came: Perrin took Sean on her lap and gave him a pile of sugar packets to play with; more food arrived for the adults; conversation resumed. But the nervousness remained, just below the surface.

Sean brought up his skin color a number of times that year. He wanted to look like everyone else in the family, wanted physical, visual proof that he belonged and could never be left out—a powerful hunger for a little boy who had already lost one family. All any of us could do was explain, over and over again, that looks don't make a family, knowing that time would prove it.

And I think it has. If Sean and I don't look alike, we certainly sound alike, much like our father, who grew up on the Lower East Side during the Great Depression and had a bit of borscht belt to him. Sean and I share the same love of dumb jokes, the same penchant for grandiose plan making, whether it's about kayaking the Atlantic or biking the continent. I was at his adoption hearing, at his big tap dance performance, at all his school graduations. My wife and I signed him up for his first photography class, a small gift that bore extravagant fruit: photography became his college major and then his profession. He paid us back by taking the pictures at my first book party. He was at our wedding, at the hospital when our oldest child, Jonah, was born, at the bris. Fifteen years ago, we stood with Perrin and David beside our father's coffin; now, when I go to New York, we all drive out to the cemetery together to visit Dad's grave and walk among the headstones, telling jokes and laughing just as our father would have.

My worry in even mentioning race is that I might end up misrepresenting our experience by focusing on something that is irrelevant to the fabric of our daily lives as siblings. The problem, however, is that silence would be equally distorting. For if race is a purely social construct, a figment of the collective imagination, a thing out *there*, on the street, not in *here*, within the family, it can bounce around in highly unpredictable ways.

Soon after Sean arrived, I took him with me to spend the day with a bunch of people at a house in Fire Island. We made a splash. He was completely outgoing, interested in everyone, full of laughter. People passed him around from arm to arm, cooing over him. Someone said to me, "This is just the most wonderful thing you're doing. You've rescued a child and given him a home. A little black boy."

That felt odd. I hated the way it flattened out the interactions between complicated individuals and turned the whole thing into an act of charity. There was no recognizing us in that. We were basically instinctual people, neither political nor principled, and more than a little selfish. "Oh no, really, it's the other way around. He's here to rescue us," I said.

"But you've changed a life."

"No, he's changed ours." I meant it, though the more calculating part of me already realized that this, too, would be taken as an expression of modesty and simply get me more kudos—which is why I said it, of course.

Indeed, as these encounters multiplied, I got over my unease and started accepting the praise, then basking in it, then expecting it, even courting it, feeling miffed when it didn't come my way. I started borrowing Sean from my parents whenever I had a social occasion where I wouldn't know many people. He was perfect for backyard barbecues in Brooklyn, picnics in Central Park. With him in my arms I stood out: I was the guy with the cute little brown brother. I would carry him around the party, introducing him to all the women, and thus introducing myself in the most flattering, if contrived, light: Mr. Sensitivity, the urban saint, but also hip, because Sean was a hip little kid with his incredible smile and wonderful ringlets.

Of course, that wasn't the only type of dynamic we had. Soon after the trip to Fire Island, we were riding downtown on a city bus when I noticed a middle-aged white woman across the aisle, watching us very closely. Sean's asthma was acting up and he was coughing, a wet, ugly chest cough that always made me upset—I hated that he had to struggle for breath. "That's a nasty cough," said the woman.

"He's got asthma," I said, feeling obscurely accused of something, some sort of negligence—or maybe it was illegitimacy.

"He should see a doctor."

"We have medicine for it."

"Mmm," she said, looking skeptical.

From that point on, I started noticing a pattern wherever we went: older white women peering to see if Sean's coat was properly zipped, if I held his hand when we crossed the street, if I let him drink from the sippy cup he'd just dropped on the sidewalk. It took me a while to realize that they didn't see the hip older brother. They assumed I was the *father.* And though I was twenty-five by then, I was the sort of baby-faced twenty-five that looked eighteen, and not particularly prosperous, either, in my repertoire of old jeans and T-shirts. Sean was still in the thrift shop clothes my parents had inherited with him, which contained an alarming number of Michael Jackson tank tops. Stuff from the bottom of the box at Goodwill. I can only imagine how these women filled in the blanks: teen parents, black and white, poor, hapless. A sort of interracial *La bohème*, with a coughing, wheezing child.

The somewhat pathetic truth is that I was secretly flattered and did nothing to dispel the impression. He had been with us almost a year, and I guess I felt a little possessive of Sean by that point, but there was more to it: fatherhood was grown-up, and nothing else about my life felt that way. I was working part-time as a Japanese-speaking tour guide, living with a roommate, and writing nothing worth keeping, but I walked a little straighter when I had him with me.

Toward the end of Sean's first year with us, the legitimacy of our connection was challenged from outside. I got a call from my mother, who told me that an organization of African American social workers had weighed in on Sean's adoption. Its interest wasn't Sean's case specifically, but the broader issue of adoption policy; it believed that African American kids should go to African American families, and it asked some cogent questions: How would black children raised in white homes understand their African American heritage? How would they learn how to navigate the difficulties of race in America without African American role models?

I could see that they had a point; I just wanted them to make it using someone else's adoption. My parents got worried. They were receiving regularly scheduled home visits from social workers as the adoption process continued. What if policy changed and the agency started recommending against transracial adoptions? "He's half white," said my father. "Why isn't he considered white? I mean, why choose one half rather than the other?"

"Look at his skin," my mother said.

"He looks like he got a tan at the beach." That was pretty much true. Sean's biological father was African American, but his biological mother was Caucasian. His biological half brothers all had Caucasian fathers and looked positively Nordic, with blond hair and blue eyes.

"You're not being practical," said my mother.

But my father was stuck on his point. "He's not black or white. He's a harlequin, black *and* white."

"That's idiotic."

My parents, never much into preparation, made an effort to forestall any possible criticism. They started dressing Sean in a dashiki for big occasions such as Passover and Yom Kippur. We all made a halfhearted effort to celebrate Kwanzaa, right after Hanukkah, getting instructions from a book.

The adoption started to get a little messy for other reasons. Sean's mother had abandoned the boys in the middle of their brother's abuse case; she'd run away to Puerto Rico with a janitor from the homeless shelter they lived in, and my parents were worried that she would return to contest his adoption. If she did, there wouldn't be a chance of winning;

he would have to go back to her. My parents talked about this possibility at night, when Sean was asleep, during long, circular discussions. "She let the other three go," said my father.

"She's unpredictable," said my mother.

"She won't come back."

"She might."

She didn't; what happened is that my mother's agency realized that Sean had been tangentially connected to the abuse case my mother had prosecuted a couple of years back, involving his brother with the broken arm. The agency brought up the possibility of what it called "the appearance of impropriety." What they were worried about was a tabloid headline something like "City Lawyer Steals Kid from Mom, Legally!" My mother was called in to talk to her boss, and then to her boss's boss. She was passed over for a promotion that had once looked like a sure thing and then transferred out of the courts altogether, to a job doing paperwork. The inspector general's office brought her up on a battery of charges, some of which were pretty far-flung—an effort to find something that would stick.

This new twist was especially frightening for my parents: now that my father was in what was delicately called "semiretirement," my mother's job was their primary support. But what really concerned them was the potential impact on the adoption. My father would get worked up into long, dramatic rants. "I'll never hand him over," he told me. "I'll take him and go on the lam."

"Does anyone even say *lam* anymore?" I asked, trying to lighten the mood.

"I'll change my name and drive out west. They'll never find us."

"Isn't that called kidnapping?"

"Who cares what it's called."

I don't know if my father was afraid that his legal troubles would come out and affect the adoption; he never mentioned it. But I couldn't help feeling that he had been looking for reasons to go on the lam for years before Sean arrived, anyway. He often fantasized about radical personal transformation: living on a sailboat, opening a bookstore in Vermont.

And yet I also understood his sense of crisis. Sean had taken root inside our hearts; whatever the law said, there was no disentangling him now.

THE CHARGES AGAINST MY mother were eventually dropped; the adoption went through. Yet a sense of insecurity stayed with us for years afterward. Would Sean have been better off in an African American family? A younger family with more energetic parents and siblings closer in age? Part of this was a reaction to the bumpiness of the adoption process, part of it just a by-product of who we are: overly ruminative, insecure people. But there was something more, too: a sense of the willfulness of choosing a little boy still too young to choose you back. Sure, he seemed to love us, all right, but given the opportunity, would he have *chosen* us? This question, fundamentally unanswerable, was more an expression of anxiety than anything else. No one frets over the fact that biological children don't choose their families. But irrational or not, it lingered.

Five or six years after the adoption went through, the entire family was in my parents' Japanese station wagon, making a slow arc around the concrete island at the center of Times Square. Traffic was snarled and we crept along, only slowly becoming aware of a commotion on the center island. Someone was shouting through an old PA system, and though it was hard to make out every word, we could all understand enough to know that he was very, very angry. *Jew* was one of the few words that cut through the distortion.

An African American man stood on a portable stage, a microphone in his hand. He was dressed like the genie in *Aladdin*, in a turban, a sash, and the trademark puffy pants, and behind him stretched a line of other African American men dressed in the same style, looking determined and scary despite the harem pants. A banner read THE TWELVE TRIBES OF ISRAEL. "The Jews have stolen everything from us," said the man with the microphone. "Not just our freedom but our identity. *We* are the true Israelites. Not them. Us!" He had a lot to say about Jewish bloodsuckers, slave masters, bankers, and pawnbrokers, but what got me was not the anti-Semitic rhetoric so much as the look on Sean's face as he listened next to me: confused, guarded, bruised.

The smart thing would have been to respond with something right away, something about how crazy these people were, how they didn't matter, how families can be black and white, Jewish and not-Jewish, how they can be anything they want to be as long as the people in them love each other. Instead, we all sat very still, trying to act as if nothing were happening while we willed the light to turn so we could escape.

It was Sean who finally spoke. "They're not talking to me."

Over the next couple of years, Sean took tap dancing lessons and tap danced in the living room as we sat on the couch, a wryly captive audience. He got a video camera and created movie trailers to nonexistent movies. We would line up chairs and eat popcorn as we watched them on the TV, discussing everything that happened off-screen. After a trip to Disney World, he developed a fear of flying, which he remedied by obsessively watching airplane documentaries on cable TV. When I came over, he would explain the intricacies of airspeed, engine thrust, lift, and the rigors of aerospace engineering. "The wings can bend thirty degrees in either direction, up or down," he said, showing me with his arms. "That's how strong they are." Once, he walked in the door with our father; they had spent the afternoon at LaGuardia Airport, watching the planes take off. "Takeoff is the trickiest time," Sean explained.

"Yes, but there's something beautiful about watching them angle up into the sky," said my father.

"Flying is safer than driving, and we drive every day," said Sean. "There's nothing to be afraid of."

My father smiled. He was fragile and often afraid of what life seemed to require of him, but not in those moments.

From Sean, I learned that family is not defined by blood. It is not defined by race. It is not even defined by a shared voice or way of telling a story. Family is who you choose to love. The unfathomable complexity of those two terms, *choose* and *love*, starts to feel simple after a while, when you live them day by day.

THREE YEARS AFTER WE got stuck in Times Square with the Twelve Tribes of Israel, when Sean was ten, I moved in with Karen, the woman I would eventually marry. It was an experiment in those same two words, *choose* and *love*. Karen worked on her novel in the bedroom, I worked on mine in the living room, and on days when we were both stuck and frustrated, we would switch: I would write hers, and she would write mine. And yet in other moments, the act of sharing a life together still felt tentative, fragile. Where should that vase go in the living room? How best to wash and dry the dishes? What did it mean to say, *Ours*?

One day, Karen said, "I've been thinking that we should have Sean over."

"You mean a sleepover?"

I remember him arriving at our house with his overnight stuff in his school bag, formal and shy and very pleased. We made dinner together, and talked, and soon it was time to go to bed. He slept on the couch. We tucked him in and watched him sleep, amazed at his presence in our home, the home we were constructing together. The next day, we walked him to school, full of the importance of our task: *Sean has to be at PS3 by eight o'clock, sharp, he can't be late.* I remember walking up the steps with him, pulling open the big front door and catching a glimpse of the world inside, kids' projects taped to the walls, a rich and complex world that was entirely unknown to us, *his*. "Bye," he said.

"Wait, shouldn't we go in with you?" I asked. "I mean, walk you to your classroom?"

"No," he said simply, and sailed in.

The big door closed behind him, and Karen and I stood on the school steps, at a momentary loss. Was this okay? Were we forgetting something? How could he leave us like this? I think part of the confusion was how large the world was becoming, how many concentric rings it was proving to have: first Sean, then Karen. What might happen next?

Our oldest child, Jonah, was born in 1999, while we were living in an apartment in Tribeca, right beside the Hudson River. Sean was fifteen then, a big, burly teenager, already a head taller than anyone else in the family, but he held the baby with a natural, unselfconscious gentleness that I had never seen in a young man. And he was genuinely interested, too: as Jonah grew, Sean would come over and play with him for hours. Eventually we hired him to do a little babysitting in the apartment, so my wife and I could get some work done or just get some rest. He learned to feed, change, bathe, and burp, learned how to take away a breakable thing with one hand while offering a toy with the other, and in the process became such an important part of Jonah's life that the mere sight of his uncle in the doorway would make our son start to laugh and clap.

In time, we got up our courage and sent them outside together: Jonah's first foray into the world beyond the apartment without his parents. It felt momentous. I secured him in the snuggly that Sean wore on his front (have you ever seen a teenage boy comfortably wearing a snuggly?), double-checked the bottle, and then watched them disappear out the door. I remember the long wait at the window till they appeared on the street, ten stories below. I remember my wife leaning against me, watching, too. I remember them crossing the West Side Highway to the river and continuing on to the newly renovated pier, with its hot dog stand and benches. The pier was surprisingly narrow from the height of our apartment, surrounded on three sides by the muscular, glistening river, and on our side by the cityscape, with its tall buildings, its rushing cars. They were tiny figures out there, but I could see Sean's arms wrapped around Jonah in the snuggly. My brother, carrying my son.

The Window

WE CAN BE TALKING about anything at all and my mother will suddenly interrupt with a particular story about me and my father—always the same story, told the same way:

Once, when I was a baby, she came in the room to find him holding me up to the window so I could hammer the glass. In other words, I had a hammer, was holding it with my two hands, and though I didn't quite have the strength to smash the pane, I was getting close; it was audibly vibrating: *clink, clink, clink.*

"Stop," she said to him. "What are you doing?"

"He's hammering," my father said.

Clink, clink, clink.

"It's dangerous."

"But he *wants* to."

Clink, clink, clink.

With that, the story always ends. "He was an exceedingly odd man, but boy, did he love you." And then she goes on with whatever she was saying before.

HOW I LEARNED TO BE A WRITER

I WANTED TO BE A writer. I wanted to suffer loneliness and rejection till I became interesting enough to hold people's attention. I wanted to create perfect sentences that would make people lean forward and listen. I wanted my sacrifices to be instantly rewarded with fame and money, and I wanted to look down on fame and money as if they were as natural as breathing. I wanted to eat dinner late at night at one of the downtown spots I read about in magazines where you had to be known to get a table. I had an anachronistic interest in Elaine's, where Woody Allen went, not realizing it wasn't a happening spot anymore. I wanted to go to parties at *The Paris Review* and feel as if I belonged, as if it weren't a pretentious and self-conscious thing to do.

Anything to counteract the ocean of sadness that felt as if it would drown me.

The problem was that I didn't know how to write, so I went to writing school to learn. On the first day, I found that the other students were extremely smart people who also, weirdly, looked like models. They had the best repartee in the world. The zingers shot through the air in the designated smoking room all day, which was thick with haze. They were always there and never seemed to go home; they sat all day in the exact same chairs in front of the ashtray, in postures of refined bemusement. But then when it was their turn to submit work to class they handed out stories of great beauty.

How was this possible? I would pull all the stories from the workshops and read them, burning with envy and confusion. I would go back to my apartment and lie in bed wondering what was wrong with me. And then I would sit in front of my clunky desktop computer with the green writing on the screen and wait for inspiration to strike, until the waiting became unbearable and I jumped up and began pacing the apartment.

It turned out that I would do anything to become a writer except write. Actually putting words on the page gave me a terrible feeling as if I had inadvertently, in a moment of forgetfulness, pressed a button that would destroy the world. I would have a seizure of terror, and then feel sad and guilty and intensely nostalgic for the time before I killed everyone. I would squeeze my eyes shut and then open them again to see the world still there, undestroyed. But even then the feeling didn't go away; it just started over again with the next sentence.

The problem was that I was trying to write a novel about what happened to my father—to us. When my father, a criminal defense lawyer, went to jail, it had destroyed us. I remember wanting to exonerate him, justify him, remove his pain. I wanted to express my anger and love. But I felt guilty and ashamed for even mentioning it, and this crosscurrent made it impossible to say anything.

What I think I secretly wanted was to be the kind of person who *could* write, who wasn't afraid of speaking. And I wanted to take this terrible experience and profit from it, make it something good.

It was just when the money was, in fact, running out, and my sense of panic was going from hypothetical to real, that I got a call from a Korean American woman I knew at college. Her father was a professor of Korean Buddhism, a former Buddhist monk, who wanted to start a publishing company to produce scholarly books on Korean religions. But he didn't know anything about publishing and needed help. Was I interested in a job?

"I don't know anything about publishing, either."

"You're a writer," she said. "You lived in Japan. And you're the only person I can think of who might possibly get along with my father."

A few days later, Prof. Park picked me up outside of my apartment building in Manhattan and drove us to a Korean barbecue place somewhere deep in Queens, a large smoky hall where no English seemed to be spoken. We sat opposite each other, wearing bibs.

"Robert," he said, with a wonderfully formal manner possessed only by foreign speakers who have mastered the language from outside and know it as a thing of elegance and beauty. "I have asked you here today because we are in a time of *crisis*."

Crisis was something I definitely understood. I liked Prof. Park already: his sense of occasion, and the way he gave a slow snap to certain words, as if they were bones and he was breaking them open to eat the marrow.

"Korean religious studies in America are in the most extreme *danger*," he continued. "A new generation of American scholars has completely misunderstood the fundamental nature of Korean Buddhism, and they are spreading their false views throughout the academy. They treat it as if it were a *philosophy*, a collection of clever ideas like structuralism or postmodernism, and not a *religion*. They do not understand that Buddhism is about *salvation*. He put down the spare rib in his hands and wiped his fingers on his bib. "Robert, the world needs salvation. That is why I must risk everything to save Korean Buddhist studies in America. But I can't do it alone—I don't have the strength." He pantomimed exhaustion, slumping his shoulders as if under a great weight.

"How can I help?" I asked.

"I can't communicate with most Americans so easily. But you're different. You *understand*."

I looked over at Prof. Park, across the table with its smoky brazier and many plates. He looked to be in his early fifties, about the age my father was when he first came under investigation and our world began to shift and crack beneath us. "I'll take the job," I said.

"I'm glad to hear that." He reached into the old leather satchel on the floor by his chair and handed me a copy of his book, *Buddhist Faith and Sudden Enlightenment*. "Now we must begin your education."

Back at home, I stayed up till dawn reading that beautiful little book, unable to put it down. *Buddhist Faith* is about the battle between faith and doubt, and the central role of faith in the Buddhist enlightenment process. As Prof. Park describes it, Korean Son Buddhism believes that Great Doubt, the beginner's fear that he or she will never reach enlightenment, can't simply be replaced with the standard tenet of Buddhist belief, the idea that "in fact there's nothing to reach, because you are already a perfect Buddha." There needs to be an intermediary step first, a bridge. That bridge is called "Patriarchal Faith," meaning faith in the Patriarchs, the generations of practitioners who achieved enlightenment ahead of you. Son practitioners are taught to believe in the Patriarchs first, until the act of faith becomes so deeply rooted in them that it doesn't need an explanation or object: it just *is*.

Though I'd studied Japanese literature and lived in Japan, I'd always had minimal tolerance for Buddhist theory: it was too dry for me, too abstract. Looking back, I think Prof. Park's book just happened to map onto my current situation with uncanny precision: on the one hand, I absolutely had to write my novel; on the other hand, I absolutely had to *not* write it. I saw no way of leaping over that contradiction and had stopped believing that I ever would. All I could envision was continuing just as I was, writing and erasing, occasionally stopping by my parents' apartment to see if my father was answering his office phone as himself rather than an imaginary secretary.

And that was the big difference between my world and the world described in Prof. Park's book: I had no one to put my faith in. The closest thing I had to a Patriarch, my father, was a strange and melancholy disaster who sat at home much of the day, eating great quantities of leftovers and downing antidepressants.

Working for Prof. Park distracted me from my stuckness. In his office, I sat at a little desk next to his big one and wrote elaborate letters for him in his formal style, the sort of ornately polite correspondence not seen since the advent of the telephone. Most of those letters were written for other people, pawns in various schemes he was cooking up to save Korean religious studies. We wrote them for the president of the university to use, thanking one or another donor in Korea for his or her generous support. We wrote letters for those donors to send back to the president, reiterating their belief in the urgency of our mission and hinting at a desire to donate even more, if the university would only increase its support, too. We wrote letters for various Korean scholars to send to the donors *and* the president, expressing their belief that the Korean Studies Publication Project would change the direction of scholarship in the U.S. In each case, Prof. Park would put a copy of the letter in a file he was keeping, "for the record." Someone reading that file would have thought there was a vast network of extremely ceremonious people out in the world, deeply worried about the fate of Korean religious studies, but also quietly hopeful, if only we act now.

When we ran out of letters to write, Prof. Park would lean back in his big chair and talk about Buddhism. These weren't conversations so much as beautiful monologues, rhapsodies, incredibly fluent, passionate, grand. I would put down my pen, forgetting the manuscripts that still needed editing, feeling an odd sense of peace settle over me—completely unaware of how the moment recalled other moments, long gone, when I would sit in my father's office and watch him entertain clients with stories about the criminal courts. I was too young to really understand those stories, which were twisty, dark, absurdist. But I had total faith in the message encoded in his voice, which seemed to imply that only he knew how to keep us all safe. The more complicated and bewildering the things he described, the safer I always felt.

As Prof. Park talked, the light from the big window behind him would start to drop, turning the room golden and melancholy, and I would give up on catching the five p.m. train back to the city. I had a sense that he was lonely and didn't want to go home, and on some level that was okay with me, because the only thing waiting back in New York was my novel, with all its unfinished sentences.

And then one evening he called me up at home, where I was at the computer, painstakingly erasing lines from the novel. "Robert, I am afraid I need your help." He explained that he had a paper due at the end of the week for a conference on interfaith dialogue and he hadn't been able to get to it. "Sometimes I get so busy helping others that I forget to help myself." He gave a pained laugh, and then launched immediately into a hyper-articulate discussion of Jesus and Buddha and how they were really one and the same. "Can you edit that for me?"

"Email me some text and I'll whip it into shape."

"There isn't time. Just write it exactly as I said it."

"Prof. Park, you forget that I don't really know anything about Buddhism."

"I trust you." He hung up before I could properly object.

I hadn't taken any notes, and the words now hovered in the silence, just out of reach of my memory. What remained was the resonance of his voice, the mixture of wonder and excitement and delight in his own smartness that was the essence of Prof. Park. I began to write, imagining that I was at the little desk in his office, and that he was at the big desk, dictating, as we did with the letters. And then, as I gained momentum, things blurred and I was sort of me and sort of him, speaking and listening, grabbing the words out of the stillness of the room, which is how I first became at least semi-aware that there might be some use to forgetting who held the pen.

One of our authors, a Korean professor working at a university in the Washington area, was sending us chapters as he completed them, racing to finish the manuscript in time for tenure—when suddenly the chapters stopped coming, and Prof. Park told me, "You need to go down there and finish it for him."

"But I can't do that." I had my own book to write. I didn't want to lose the delicate sense of forward motion, of possibility.

"If he doesn't finish, he won't get tenure, and if he doesn't get tenure, he'll lose his job. We can't let that happen."

Prof. Park imagined himself the éminence grise of Korean religious studies in the U.S. He had a network of younger Korean academics whom he watched, prodded, nurtured. One thing the Korean Studies Publication Project did was publish their first books and help them get tenure.

I took Amtrak from Penn Station to somewhere in suburban Maryland, got off, and walked down the stairs to the parking lot, where the professor was supposed to be waiting for me. We'd never met before, but spotting him was easy because he was the only Asian around: A short, stocky Korean man in a raincoat buttoned to the neck, smoking a pipe.

"Robert Siegel?" he asked.

"That's me."

We drove to one of those magically odd subdivisions where a single house has replicated itself everywhere in slightly altered shapes, and thus seems to imply that you are not awake but dreaming. His wife met us at the door, a very small Korean woman dressed in surgical scrubs. She was an operating room nurse who assisted in ocular surgery, and she had the brisk, no-nonsense air of someone who handles tiny knives meant for eyeballs. I could tell right away that she was deeply irritated with the professor—irritated that he had fucked up and needed someone to rescue him. As if to drive the point home, she sat me down in the living room and had their little boy play Chopin on the piano. He was maybe ten years old, pear shaped, with a crew cut and complicated, intelligent eyes, and his small chubby fingers flew over the keys.

"Pretty good, no?" she said to me.

"Marvelous," I answered.

"He practices every day."

The professor seemed to feel their dual judgment acutely, and as a result his expression grew more and more pompous and dignified. He had a beard but no mustache; his upper lip was shaved and looked bare and vulnerable. It made him seem like an old-time ship's captain out of Melville, the kind with vast knowledge of scripture and a tragic sense of the future.

"Come," he said to me. "Let me show you to your room."

He took me up to the attic, which had been renovated into a small guest room but still had the low, sloping ceiling that made you aware of the roof's curvature, its roofiness.

"You'll see I have an outline and notes for you to use," he said, pointing to a thick folder on the desk by the bed. "And all the English sources I've been citing." Beside the desk were two stacks of books bristling with Post-its.

"That's great," I said. "This should be no problem."

"Writing in English was hard, but I thought I could make it to the end." He looked distressed, which for him meant intensely dignified, but with an unhinged glint in the eyes.

"Well, you got most of the way," I said, trying to reassure him. "That's pretty awesome."

"But then something happened. I sat for days, unable to write the next sentence. What do you call that, writer's block?"

"Yes, writer's block," I said.

"Not even a single sentence," he said, sounding bewildered.

I spent almost two weeks in that attic, writing the professor's book for him. Mornings I would type as fast as I could, using his outline and notes and quotes from the volumes stacked by the desk. Afternoons, he and I would take long walks through the subdivision, discussing the material, which was full of complicated numerical schemata in keeping with neo-Confucian metaphysical commentary: the four elements and six principles, the nine essences and twelve signs. Most interesting to me was the view of language itself, the belief that it was a mystical force with the power to shape reality, something like a magic spell. Use the right words in the right way, and nations would become prosperous, families happy.

"What do you think of that?" I asked the professor.

He had his raincoat buttoned up to the neck as he trudged along, smoking his pipe. "They didn't know about writer's block back then."

The midwinter light was falling, turning the street a dark shade of purple. Since the houses all looked more or less the same, we could have walked into any one of them and been home, for all I knew. The result was an inexplicable nostalgia that grew more intense each time we turned a corner, and somehow reminded me of a time in my boyhood when my family moved from one apartment building to another a few blocks away. Each time I passed our old building, I would get the same sort of overpowering feeling, and would have to force myself to keep walking to the place we now lived.

That evening, as always, I ate with the professor's family and then listened to the little boy play the piano in the living room. The professor sat in an armchair, reading what I had produced that day and jotting down comments while the music flowed over us, a beautiful reproach. And then I headed upstairs to work through the night, cradled by the sloping ceiling and the pool of light around my desk, high above the rest of the world.

The truth was that I actually liked writing the professor's book. Sitting at the desk, I would picture that grave, pompous, wounded face, and then pretend it was my face, that I was him, and suddenly, without effort, the sentences would start to unfurl.

My trip to Maryland came to a close. I finished the professor's book and packed my bag. His wife and son were downstairs to say goodbye. I asked the boy to play something and he did, something complicated and fast, a torrent of exquisite notes coming from those tiny fingers.

The professor's wife stuffed a thick wad of cash in my hand. "This is from me," she said, looking friendly for the first time. "Something extra."

I didn't know what I thought about the money—a tip, essentially. Imitating a Korean neo-Confucianist was not at all like fixing the bathroom sink. But I liked the bulky heft of the bills in my palm.

"You'll miss your train," said the professor, picking up my bag and carrying it out to the car, his raincoat buttoned to the top, as always. I followed, the music flowing out the door behind me.

Back in New York, my novel started to go a little better. Maybe it was just the time away, but what stuck in my mind was the experience of pretending to be the professor. Sitting at the computer at home, I would imagine myself hovering above the ground, almost as if I were still in his attic, but this time so high up that my characters looked tiny, and their sorrow and stupidity nothing to be afraid of. Then I would imagine that my arms were incredibly long, miles long, reaching all the way down to my keyboard. Typing from so far above, it was almost as if I wasn't typing at all. I started to finish my sentences.

About this time, I was pulled into a sort of side project, writing emails for yet another Korean professor, who was carrying on an affair with a woman in Queens. I'd met this other professor's wife and little daughter, and I didn't want to be a part of whatever process was working itself out. But when I tried to beg off, his face turned furious. "Don't judge me, Robert," he said.

Judgment? My father was an ex-con, and I was writing a book about him behind his back, detailing his greatest humiliations, and hoping to sell it to the public. I stared at my hands, feeling my face burn.

"It's a lot more complicated than you think," said this professor—I will call him Professor X. "I'm trying to figure out my future."

Every couple of days, I'd sit at his computer with him, working out a reply to her latest—which was odd, since the woman was clearly Korean. What was the point of writing in English? And why did he need me to make his emails better, given that hers remained just the same as before, utterly sprawling and completely ungrammatical? I felt too conflicted to ask those sorts of questions, but the possibilities resonated as we strategized his answer in front of the screen, typing and erasing and retyping, printing out draft after draft before finally hitting send. The whole thing felt perilously fictional to me, by which I mean not unreal, but delicately and obsessively imagined, like Prof. Park's campaign to save Korean religious studies—or like my novel.

"I'm thinking of telling her that I can't leave my wife, after all," said Professor X, his knee nervously bouncing up and down. "There's my daughter to consider."

"Excellent idea. Let me write that."

"But I think it's better to hint first, so she gets used to the idea. I don't want to make her upset."

"Okay, let me put in a subtle hint here."

He stood up suddenly, as if he'd gotten an electric shock. "But Robert, what if I'm missing my one chance at happiness?"

"It's incredibly complicated, I know."

A part of me quite liked being Professor X on the Internet for a few hours in the afternoon, as the falling light slanted in and the sky began to darken. There was something about the idea that your feelings were urgent and important simply because they were your feelings, that your pleasure and happiness mattered more than anything—it left me wistful and a little dazed. Back at home, I was trying to work on the novel's prison chapters, but the little mental trick of placing myself in the Maryland professor's attic no longer helped get me past my own internal resistance. In real life, I'd been living in Japan when my father went to prison and I had completely missed that entire segment of his ordeal. The fragments my mother and siblings had described made it sound hideous: long train trips to Connecticut, followed by a special prison bus, full of anxious, hard-luck families with lots of crying children. Once inside, my father would shake them down for all the spare change they'd been able to collect during the week: he used it for the vending machines at the other side of the cafeteria. After gorging on whatever he could buy from the machines, he refused to talk to them. Sometimes he'd sit for a while, looking furious and strange; other times, he'd simply walk away. He never spoke about that period. If it came up, his face would become agitated and he'd fall silent.

It's a novel, I told myself. *Make it up. That's what you're supposed to do with novels.* But somehow I just couldn't. My father's time in prison appeared to me like a box full of sorrow so overwhelming it could not be opened, a toxic mixture of all of our vanity and stupidity and pretension and naïveté and blindness. If I were to lift the lid, something unimaginable—by which I mean irrefutably true—would pour out and drown us all.

I couldn't write a word, not even to erase it immediately after. The computer screen became a window onto darkness. I came down with a brain worm–like case of insomnia in which I went two days at a time without even closing my eyes, wandering around in a sort of endless shopping mall of wakefulness. I must have looked pretty bad, because one day at my parents' apartment, my father asked me how the novel was coming.

"My novel?" I asked.

"Yes, how's it going?"

"Not so good," I said, and then maybe because we were sitting in his shabby little makeshift office, doing his billing, I began to complain that what I really needed was an office, that if only I had a dedicated, private space in which to write, I could finish the book.

My father nodded sympathetically, but when I came back a few days later, he mentioned in passing, "Hey, listen, don't be mad, but you'll probably be getting some calls about office space."

"What do you mean?"

"Well, I had a free afternoon, so I stopped by a few buildings and talked to the management."

"And you gave them my number?" It was ridiculous; I didn't have the extra money to rent an office—didn't have the extra money to rent a square foot of an office.

"Just one thing, don't be surprised if they talk like they've met you already." He gave an embarrassed little laugh. "Because I pretended I was you."

Suddenly I had a vision of the entire city full of people pretending to be someone else, characters in novels of their own devising. "Why did you do that?" I asked, all irritation gone, only curious.

"I don't know." He looked genuinely perplexed for a moment, and then he said, "Your sister told me that your book has a prison chapter in it, and that you're stuck."

Of course, I shouldn't have been so surprised. On some level, I'd always known that he understood the novel was about him; the idea that he couldn't surmise that much was just plain stupid, a convenient fiction. And yet even now, I couldn't let that fiction go. "A prison chapter is just one possibility I'm considering," I said, feeling my heart begin to throb in my chest. "There are others."

"Well, if you do decide to write it, I've been there and can tell you whatever you need, I don't mind. Ask anything."

His face was composed as he waited, with none of the panic he'd shown at other times when the subject came up. He had clearly thought this moment over, prepared himself. But now that I had my chance, I couldn't ask anything: the questions were all buried too deep, under too many contradictory feelings. I stared down at the paperwork on the desk, listening to the blood pound through my head.

After a while he said, "Why don't I just tell you a few details," and then began with his first night at the prison camp in Danbury, Connecticut, how they put him in the infirmary because his blood pressure was explosive. He talked about the guards—screws, he called them—and how they harassed everyone all the time, strip-searching them for no reason, taking every chance to humiliate them. The screws would call them names, trying to get them to react so they could write them up for infractions. And yet the biggest problem was not the guards but the boredom. Some inmates kept busy, and others spent the entire time lying on their cots, staring at the ceiling. He got a job mowing the grass, and lost two hundred pounds. It helped that the food in the cafeteria was dreadful, and the vending machines took only coins. If you had cash, the guards would order Chinese takeout for you, for a fee, but he never had any money.

No, the worst thing wasn't the boredom or the food; it was being locked up.

"Did anyone ever try to escape?" It was more a wish than a question.

"Nobody. We were all short-timers. We just had to sit tight and wait."

I started to breathe again, slowly. Beyond anything else, it was listening to his voice, the fact that we were talking about the one thing I assumed we could never talk about and nothing cataclysmic was happening. It turned out that the box I was so frightened of opening contained only ordinary sorrow, the kind I was familiar with.

"You can use any of that," my father said, once he finished talking. "You have my permission."

His office had a glass door that led onto a long, barren balcony that no one had ever figured out how to decorate. I stepped outside, and then stood by an empty planter, letting the winter wind off the East River freeze me till the panic and the gratitude and the sense of stupidity all subsided. It was too early to wonder what this new kind of novel might look like, or who I would have to become in order to write it.

Lockjaw

Once, I was playing with a piece of sharp metal and cut myself on the hand, deep. I started to worry about tetanus, or what my mother called lockjaw. I remembered her explaining that as the infection got worse, your jaws locked shut and you starved to death; she'd read that in a novel by Flaubert. But I thought she would be mad about the piece of metal, so I decided not tell her what had happened. Instead, I walked around with my mouth wide open so at least I'd be able to eat.

FRIENDS

IN THE SUMMER OF 1980, Stephen Pfeiffer checked into a room at the Mutiny Hotel in Coconut Grove, Florida, near Miami, and began freebasing cocaine with a friend of his, a man by the name of Michael Borkin. They got so high that they started lighting twenties and throwing them up at the mirrored ceiling. They filled the hot tub with fifty thousand dollars in cash and lit it on fire, then crawled through the smoke toward the terrace. One of them dropped his silver-plated .44 along the way. Both climbed over the railing and scaled down the façade of the hotel, from terrace to terrace, twelve stories down, into the arms of police. On the following page are two news photos of the descent. In the first, the two men are nearing the end of their climb. Pfeiffer is at the top, without a shirt. In the second, the two men have reached the ground—and the police.

When he called my father, Pfeiffer was less interested in whatever legal trouble he might be in than the idea that the mafia was after him. That's why he'd burnt the money and climbed down the front of the building: to get away. He wanted my father to convince them to forgive him and let him live.

It was the summer after my freshman year of college. We were sitting at the big, round dining table in the middle of the afternoon when my

Mutiny Hotel jumpers scaling down the side of the hotel, 1980. Tim Chapman, photographer. Tim Chapman Collection, HistoryMiami Museum, 2013-334-80-36-13.

Mutiny Hotel jumpers clinging to an awning while being apprehended by law enforcement, 1980. Tim Chapman, photographer. Tim Chapman Collection, HistoryMiami Museum, 2013-334-80-36-11.

father told me this story. "The coke makes him crazy," he said, laughing fondly. He was incredibly indulgent of his clients, as if they were prodigal children.

"So what did you do?" I asked.

"I made some discrete inquiries on his behalf. And then I told him the truth, that it was all in his head."

"Did he believe you?"

"Yeah, he was already coming out of it by then."

I mostly sat around the dining room table that summer. I don't know if I'd gotten out of my pajamas since getting back from college in June. On move-in day in September, my father had dropped me off and run back to the car, weeping. And I'd stood on the corner watching him go, feeling as if I might drown. I didn't want to be around normal people, who would hate me. I wanted to be back at home, with him and the clients.

Pfeiffer had first shown up five or six years before that, when I was still in middle school. I'd come home in the afternoon, and he was sitting at the same table with my father: in his late twenties, maybe, not large but muscular, boyish, with high cheekbones and startling blue eyes that had an arctic cold to them. He looked directly at me while he talked, never shifting his gaze, as if he needed to keep an eye on me. There was something hushed about him, careful, and there was also something suppressed. It felt as if he might reach out and with a gentle but decisive pressure of his fingers crush my head.

"Your old man is a genius," he said that first day. "I've never seen anyone talk to a jury like that."

I already knew this to be true. I'd grown up sitting in the hard wooden benches of courtrooms, beneath the high ceilings and tall windows, watching my father stand up in that church-like area near the judge's platform and tell stories that made the jurors see the goodness in his clients so that they could forgive them. He would show them how appearances deceived: somebody who looked like a criminal could be an orphan, or a devoted father, or husband—an innocent man.

"It's about creating an emotional bond with the jury," said my father. "While at the same time creating reasonable doubt."

"I knew he was the only one who could win this," said Pfeiffer. "The only one in the world."

My father seemed to expand in his chair, delighted with Pfeiffer's praise. He had been going to court each morning with an unusual air of bustle, his hair brushed back, carrying a file of papers with him, and he'd just won a big acquittal for Pfeiffer at trial. Weapons charges, he'd told me.

"How'd you do it?" I asked him.

"It was simple, I just said that the machine gun wasn't his."

After that, Pfeiffer was around a lot, the living proof of my father's genius. He dropped by the apartment to chat in that incredibly polite and well-mannered way. He went out to dinner with my parents. He came to school events, graduation parties. Many years later, when my sister, Perrin, got an MFA in painting, he came to her shows, standing with a glass of white wine in a plastic cup and examining the art on the walls—always with a vague air of irony, as if this civilized undertaking were a silly fabrication he was too smart to believe in.

"He's a little bit scary, don't you think?" I said to my mother.

She looked puzzled but interested, as if this were a novel insight. "I wonder why you'd say that. He's very widely read. We were just talking about Camus."

"He's a pussycat," said my father. "Unless he's high. Then he can get a little difficult."

"And he loves fine dining," said my mother. "He's going to take us to Le Cirque."

My mother told me that Pfeiffer had grown up on the street as a runaway, which made his intelligence and culture all the more notable. But I'm not sure where she got that notion, or whether it was in fact true. More recently, someone told me he grew up in Astoria, Queens, and went to City College. The idea of the clients as orphans and runaways, wild children in need of parents, was important to us in a way that we did not ever examine. We liked seeing ourselves as the family in charge of the orphanage, full of beautiful waifs.

What I remember from those days feels dreamlike now. What I felt back then was a sort of giddy excitement: everything was good and we were happy, surrounded by grateful and loving clients. Somehow, that went side by side with a kind of nervousness or anxiety, a feeling that things weren't in fact all right and needed to be fixed. My legs were always twitching, my fingers drumming. I suffered from stomachaches, and I couldn't sleep. At odd moments, I was seized by bouts of intense, nameless sadness that made it impossible to move. At the time, I believed those episodes came and went without cause, as aimless as clouds.

Recently, another client from that time pointed me to a blog by a friend of his, a memoir of the drug trade during the '70s and '80s that includes incidents involving Pfeiffer. I read the entries with a confused melancholy made more intense by the breezy style, as if everything described were a harmless comedy. I recognized the desire to see events that way, but couldn't fully enter into that mode anymore, with its pratfalls and jokes and oh-shit twists. It was like no longer remembering a language I'd once known how to speak.

Most of all, I was struck by how much I simply didn't know back then, because I was a kid. It was as if I were walking through a huge warehouse in the dark with just a flashlight, and I was following that narrow beam, keeping my eyes on my father a few steps ahead of me, and I was unaware of what was in the vast black spaces to either side.

The blog is called *A Funny Thing Happened on the Way to the Grave*. The author says he is finally writing because the statute of limitations has passed on everything he describes. Here is the section on Pfeiffer's trial:

> So in the late 1970s and early '80s, Pfeiffer is on the scene in Manhattan, living in a downtown loft. He's taken up with a Colombian coke smuggler named Nuvia. She was, in a lot of ways, a perfect fit for him—totally fearless, completely insane, and with an incredibly loud mouth

that never stopped spewing obscenities. It was pretty funny to hear her curse people out with her Colombian accent . . . or at least it seemed funny until one day, she just disappeared.

Steve was around but Nuvia was gone. No goodbyes, no farewells, no Nuvia. Did I mention that they fought? Steve and Nuvia were two of a kind. Loud, profane, and in each other's face. And, oh yeah, they both weren't afraid of owning guns.

Until, about six months later, I get a freaky call from Dr. S [the dentist he shared with Pfeiffer and Nuvia], "I'm calling you from a payphone near my office . . . The cops were just here . . . Homicide cops . . . and they're asking me to identify a set of teeth they found in a burlap sack in Jamaica Bay along with a full set of bones."

Pfeiffer gets indicted for murder. Yes, murder.

Defended by Stanley Siegel (RIP by Alzheimer's in 2002), Pfeiffer pleads not guilty. Siegel puts on a spectacular case, proving Nuvia was smuggling coke for the Medellín Cartel, and denying that Steve had anything to do with her disappearance or subsequent reappearance in the sack in the bay. The government put on a case with neighbors testifying about frequent fights, loud verbal abuse, and Nuvia often displaying facial bruising and black eyes. They covered Steve's record, from time in prison to his dozen felony arrests that never went to trial to his paying Saltzman for her dental rebuild. After they rest, Pfeiffer actually takes the stand and testifies on his own behalf. Talk about having a brass set of balls!! He testifies and gets acquitted because they can't rule out a possible role of the cartel that she smuggled for.

Perhaps another time, I'll share some more Pfeiffer stories because there are LOTS of them. From him flying us around in a Lear to pick up cash, to him swimming the Rio Grande with a bail of Mexican on his back, to him playing the key role in a bank robbery that "sort of just happened" a few years later. And he never . . . ever . . . told me if he did it or didn't do it. Whenever her name came up, which was not frequently, he just smiled and shrugged.

I never knew any of that till now: not that it was a murder trial; not that Pfeiffer's girlfriend was the one who had been murdered. Not that they had found a bag of bones in Jamaica Bay.

PFEIFFER MOVED TO BUFFALO, but came back to New York frequently, always staying in a gigantic suite at one of the big midtown hotels. My father would pretend to scoff at the lavishness but was impressed. "It's two thousand dollars a night," I remember him saying once. "The tub looks like a swimming pool."

He would get a call late at night and say *Pfeiffer's in town, I've got to go*, and then rush out the door with a tense sort of excitement. I have no idea when he got back, or what they did together—my father always turned it into a vaguely comic story of too much food and eye-popping restaurant bills. During summers, they met at the relatively unposh yacht club on Long Island where my father kept his sailboat and sat in the restaurant, Pfeiffer firing back vodkas, my father drinking a succession of Diet Cokes. They never got on the boat, though; my father adored his boat, or the idea of it, but it was very, very big, and he could not figure out how to get it out of the marina slip without running into the other boats. For the most part, when we went out as a family, we would just picnic on the thing while it rocked at the dock, eating antipasti from an Italian delicatessen nearby.

The only time I saw the other Pfeiffer, the one I could imagine climbing down the face of the Mutiny Hotel, was at a restaurant on Long Island over the summer. We endured a long drive from Manhattan and met him in the parking lot; he emerged from a pickup truck in jeans and no shirt, a woman in a bikini top and short shorts next to him. And for some reason, we couldn't get into the restaurant. No tables, everything reserved. I remember thinking at the time that we had been blackballed. Standing around outside, discussing what to do, Pfeiffer and the woman lost interest in the problem and began making out with great gusto in a sweaty clinch. My parents shifted nervously from foot to foot. It was not the Pfeiffer who discussed Camus with my mother.

We never did have lunch. Pfeiffer had something he wanted to talk about with my father; they stood apart talking for a little while, and then my father walked back and we drove away.

Jealousy was part of what I felt during the ride back to Manhattan: the woman, the pickup truck, the naked torso. The fact that we would drive for hours just for lunch and then drive back without it, uncomplaining. But there was something more underneath, a kind of fundamental resentment: Being good was hard and thankless work; it involved loving difficult and demanding parents, carrying the burden of their expectations. Pfeiffer got away with simply being himself. It looked like a better kind of love.

When my father came under investigation by the DEA, the first thing that happened was that he lost all his clients—which is to say that he lost all those people who had once made him feel loved and needed. He had always relished the late-night phone calls, the rituals of counsel: the phone ringing, racing to pick up, giving directions—*Hang tough. Don't say anything till I get there*—pulling on his pants, a coat, shoes untied. Then off into the mysterious world of night beyond the apartment door. It had made him feel important.

Now, his former clients avoided him. If they didn't, it was because, he suspected, they were wearing a wire—and so he avoided them. His isolation became total after his release from prison. By then, I was back from two years in graduate school in Japan, studying haiku. Though we were both living in the family apartment, along with everybody else, we hardly spoke. We'd pass each other in silence. He'd watch TV much of the day, smoking. Sometimes, he'd sit in the dark, weeping. There were big prescription pill bottles all around the house: the antidepressants his psychiatrist had prescribed. He shook out a couple and then offered me the bottle.

"No, I'm good."

"Sure?" He held up the big white pill to show me. "This one makes you feel like Swiss cheese." He popped it in his mouth and then held up a different one, blue. "And this one makes you feel like you're dead."

Gallows humor? Provocation? Aside from sardonic little moments like that one, he was generally so silent that it was hard to tell what he was thinking, and yet I sensed that he was getting crazier, crumbling in silence. One day he turned to me and said that the government was out to get him and he would have to run for his life. I tried to talk him down, but he wouldn't listen to the obvious point, that the case was over and he had already served his time. His eyes were terrified.

The only connection he seemed to have with anyone was Pfeiffer: that bond had survived everything that had happened. My father called him from a pay phone downstairs, and they arranged to meet; Pfeiffer drove down from Buffalo. A day later, my father came back from that meeting carrying the old-fashioned flight bag, stuffed with money, that he hid under the shag rug. I still remember the pain of listening to his fantasy of escape: he was talking about leaving us, perhaps forever, and yet he seemed unaware of how much that would hurt me. In fact, he seemed strangely excited by the prospect, as if this were his chance to leave the past behind and become someone new, someone happy.

Sometimes, I imagine that dinner with Pfeiffer, the one where he gave my father the bag. The two of them in the Four Seasons—Pfeiffer is paying, and he likes that kind of name-brand elegance. Pfeiffer with his spooky cool, his icy blue eyes, his permanent air of irony. My father with his long hair, haphazardly brushed, wearing a sweater stretched to the limits by his bulk. He's sweating, but he can't take the sweater off because it's concealing his dirty shirt, which he's worn for a week. His hands shake from the lithium he's been prescribed, so he keeps them under the table till the food comes, then eats with a kind of self-punishing abandon. I imagine him at his gustatory worst: he uses his hands; he gnaws the bone; he wipes the empty plate with his finger. They talk little till the food is gone. And then the telegraphic conversation of two men who have known each other for almost two decades, who are used to keeping words to a minimum. I imagine Pfeiffer as coolly accepting of the story my father tells, no matter how obviously strange: after all, he is used to the way the world looks refracted through mind-bending substances. Didn't my father listen when the mafia was after him? Now is Pfeiffer's chance to return the favor. "So what are you thinking?" he asks my father.

"I need to become unfindable."

"Then here's what we can do." He sketches out the basic plan, and my father nods along as he listens. He's barely left the house in months, so the thought of riding a bus to Buffalo makes the sweat pour down his face. The rest, the idea of flying to Panama or Colombia with a new passport, is a vague, disquieting pressure in his chest. He slips a case out of his pocket and takes a pill.

They are getting up to leave, and Pfeiffer hands him the flight bag, very casually. "Oh, yeah, almost forgot. This is for you."

I'M NOT SURE WHY he decided to stay; it's very possible that he was simply too broken to leave. Instead, he invested his cash in making himself comfortable. He began coming upstairs with Styrofoam containers of Chirping Chicken, bags of McDonald's, packs of cigarettes. Later, there were other purchases, too: cashmere sweaters, fancy Italian shoes, a silver bracelet. The ability to walk into a store and say, *That*, seemed to make him calm, calmer than the antidepressants ever could. Still sitting in front of the TV all day, he looked less angry than sad. There were moments of rueful lucidity. I remember walking with him around the neighborhood and finding out that he knew all the homeless people camped out on the streets, that he not only gave them money and cigarettes but had whole conversations, notable for their complete lack of middle-class self-consciousness. I remember thinking that something had busted inside his head—in a good way—and he was now radically equal with everyone. In turn, everyone felt free to give him advice.

"How's your back, Stan?" one man asked. He had his belongings in a shopping cart.

"Better," said my father, handing him a cigarette, lighting it for him.

"You need to walk more."

"I need to throw out the TV."

"Get the license back yet?" He meant my father's law license; he had a hearing coming up, at which I was supposed to testify, along with his psychiatrist. His lawyers were hopeful.

"I'm working on it."

He talked to Pfeiffer sometimes, too, I assume, though I don't know for sure. I'd gotten an apartment in Brooklyn and was living on my own—a place at the ungentrified end of Prospect Park, near Green-Wood Cemetery, with a window that looked out on the park's dense foliage. I was sitting at that window one night when my mother called. "You have a credit card, right?" she asked.

"Yeah, I do."

"Then you need to go to dinner with your father tonight."

"I've eaten," I said. It was after eight.

"No, you don't get it." Her voice was anxious. "He's taking Steve Pfeiffer out, but he doesn't own a credit card. You need to go with him and use your credit card."

"Why don't you use cash?" I asked.

"We don't have any."

The bag was finally empty. I felt an oppressive weight in my stomach, heaviness between my eyes, but I got up and took the subway to my parents' place, picked up my father, and went with him to the restaurant, which was obviously astoundingly expensive. We met Pfeiffer there. I hadn't seen him in a long time, and I was surprised how much older he looked. The wolflike glamour was gone. He was soft and paunchy, wearing a golf shirt: a guy from Buffalo, *middle-aged*. The waiter sized us up with a glance and ignored us.

The people at the other tables seemed to glitter. I sat with a soda, feeling comically poor. We were lowlifes, two ex-cons and a tour guide, somebody who carried around a little red flag and told outrageous lies about the monuments and buildings we passed.

Pfeiffer, who was never pretentious, took it in stride. "If you don't order wine in a place like this, they don't take you seriously."

"So order a bottle," said my father.

"Will you have some?"

"You know I don't drink."

My father's eyes were basically terrified, as if he were on a roller coaster climbing the track toward the big drop. His hands trembled, the effect of his medication accentuated by nerves. Pfeiffer said something and he laughed way too loud. It dawned on me that he didn't want to be alone with him: the real reason I was there was to act as a buffer and an excuse. Pfeiffer kept getting paged throughout the meal; he'd look at the number and then leave for the pay phone. Each time he left, my father looked at me nervously, as if I might abandon him.

I believed the part about the credit card, but felt it didn't stop there: I was serving some other purpose, too. They talked around me, very delicately. I listened, remembering how coded these conversations had always felt to me, no different now than when I was a little boy. They gossiped about people I didn't know, but my father kept switching the subject back to the food, as if he wanted to avoid going deeper. "I'm not sure what I think of these potatoes. Here, try this." He pushed his plate toward Pfeiffer.

"I like them. You can taste the truffles," said Pfeiffer.

I thought about the flight bag. Back then, I had been terrified that my father would leave us, so terrified that I had been unable to think coherently, had walked around in a sort of trance. It was a fear like drowning, the fear that I would be washed away. There were moments when that viewpoint had reversed and I was frightened for *him*, that *he* was the one who would drown. I'd imagined him going insane and ending up a homeless person on the street in a foreign country. Still other times, I'd worried that he'd go into business with Pfeiffer.

At the end of the meal, I paid with my credit card and we got up to go. "Must get this young man home," my father said, as if I were ten years old. He didn't want Pfeiffer pulling him on to another stop.

I can see now that he was trying, very tentatively, to figure out some new and better way to walk between the clients and the law, the past and the present, his need to be loved and his fear of going too far in order to earn that love.

SEVEN YEARS LATER, IN the fall of 1993, I found my father sitting on a bench outside his apartment building, with his tie undone. I sat beside him, because I knew he'd gone up to Buffalo to say a final goodbye to Pfeiffer, who was dying of lung cancer. "How did it go?" I asked.

He stared off at the traffic, looking dazed. "He died."

"But you made it in time?"

"Yeah."

He had flown up to Buffalo, he told me, with Abe Dickoff, another former client, and they had found Pfeiffer's house surrounded by tall grass, looking more or less abandoned. Nobody answered the bell, but the door was unlocked, so they walked in. The interior was a shambles, filthy; there was a horrendous smell. My father called out, got no answer, but he could sense someone present, lurking. And then he looked down and saw Pfeiffer crawling across the floor toward them, a skeleton covered in feces and bedsores. Dickoff picked him up and carried him to his bed. My father got a towel and cleaned him off. He was burning with fever, in extreme pain.

"Where was his wife?" I asked.

"I kept calling but she didn't answer."

They were trying to figure out a plan when the front door opened and a man walked in; he seemed to have the run of the place, called himself a friend of Steve's, and said he was helping take care of him. He seemed to know the wife, too. But when there were too many questions he got nervous and then quickly left.

My father found a card for a hospice taped to the wall and called the number. The nurse on the other end arranged for an ambulance and then told him to give Pfeiffer some morphine to take care of the pain: a month's supply had been dropped off just a few days earlier. But neither my father nor Dickoff could find it, and Pfeiffer suffered until the ambulance came and moved him to the hospice, where he died late the following day; my father and Dickoff got the news halfway back to New York.

But before that, on Sunday morning, they had finally reached Pfeiffer's wife, who met them at a diner by the interstate. She said she had a friend taking care of Pfeiffer during the day while she worked; she didn't know where he'd gone off to.

"That makes no sense," I said, thinking of the wrecked house, the missing morphine.

"Her arms were covered in track marks."

"They were basically holding him prisoner for his morphine," I said.

"Yeah, it seems that way." He stared off at traffic.

He never brought it up again, not once during what would turn out to be the last decade of his life. That was an incredibly rare thing for him, because he was usually an obsessive talker, someone who circled back. I tried mentioning Pfeiffer a couple of times, but my father gave me a certain rueful, pouchy-eyed look that always shut me up and made me question my own motives. Why did I want to rub it in? Because Pfeiffer had intimidated me when I was a kid and I had resented it? Because I had been jealous of the semipaternal attention he and the other clients got? Because the clients had eventually pulled us out into treacherous waters, like an undertow working at our legs? I thought about it a great deal, brooded about it. The clients had been our superheroes, but it was ending all wrong. Big Vinnie Girolama, the Hells Angel with LOVE and HATE tattooed on his knuckles, died in a holding cell after a fight with police. There was a memorial mural on the blank wall facing the clubhouse with his name and dates and the motto WHEN IN DOUBT KNOCK 'EM OUT! I would pass by now and then, sometimes not even aware that I was walking down Third Street until I saw the clubhouse, the line of choppers, the mural. At times, the mural would work the way it was supposed to and make me wistful, sentimental; other times I would wonder how we could have let ourselves believe in a mirage. And then I would think about Pfeiffer: Pfeiffer giving my father a flight bag full of money after he got out of prison; years later, my father rescuing him from that house in Buffalo so he could die in peace.

When I sat down to write this, it made me nervous that I had only my father's account of what had happened in Buffalo, based on just a single conversation, so I decided to ask Abe Dickoff for his version. He wrote me a letter:

> It was in the spring, Stanley called me and as soon as I heard his voice I knew it was time for us to go to Buffalo. We flew to Buffalo the very next day. My friend Stanley is a complex person. But we silently always understood each other and could sense what each other was thinking. I couldn't tell what Stanley was thinking or feeling this day.
>
> We arrived at Pfeiffer's address. A quiet neighborhood. Rang the bell, banged on the door, but got no response. We considered calling the police but instead I pushed my way through the front door and climbed the staircase to apartment 1. I knocked and knocked but no response. The door was unlocked and we entered. I heard that unmistakable voice say, Who's that, from the living room area but saw nobody. As I entered, I saw a body with Pfeiffer's voice. He was naked, lying on the couch, covered in feces and moaning in pain. Stanley took over the conversation while I went to the kitchen to find soap and towels. I had to clean him up. He looked worse than a Holocaust prisoner and was in excruciating pain. I cleaned him up and he adamantly refused to let us dress him or call for assistance. It took hours of crying and negotiating with Pfeiffer to allow us to dress him. Stanley found paperwork for a hospice that was trying to get him to come to their facility. I then found remnants of large pain package patches, all empty. He told us that his so-called close friends took his heroin pain patches and left him to die. Horrifying. I dressed him but couldn't move him. The pain was too much for him. Stanley called the hospice and told them what we had found. They recommended that we transport him to their facility, they couldn't give us any more pain patches. I carefully lifted him but his screaming only got louder. Step by step to the staircase and out in the car. I laid him across the back seat. Stanley

called his ex-wife and told her to meet us at the hospice. Upon arrival I carried him into the facility and was directed to a room and gently laid him down. I was asked to leave for a few minutes. Upon Stanley and myself returning, he was heavily sedated, talking slowly, opening and closing his eyes in and out of sleep or consciousness not sure about that.

It wasn't more than ten minutes when a nurse asked us to leave so Pfeiffer could rest. The nurse checked his vitals, turned to us and said he had passed on. Stanley wobbled to a chair in the room and wept. I kissed Pfeiffer's forehead and went to hug Stanley. He was distraught and had no words, which is rare for Mr. Siegel. We left the room with no direction or idea on what to do next. In the lobby was his ex-wife with Pfeiffer's twelve-year-old daughter who was the princess he always talked about. Stanley excused himself to the men's room to wash up and gather himself. I sat with his daughter and his ex-wife for a few minutes and explained the short story. Stanley arrived and gently delivered the news. I fabricated a story of his last words that included his daughter and son.

Stanley and I delicately turned the mood from sorrow to admiration about how brave Pfeiffer was till the end. I suggested we go to dinner now before our flight. The four of us went to Ruby Tuesday's and laughed at all the great moments had by all of us just knowing Steve. I excused myself for a moment, went next door to a bank, and withdrew $500 and an envelope. I gave it to his daughter stating your dad asked me to give you this. She cried and your dad reassured them we would take responsibility in making arrangement for his funeral.

Upon our return to NYC, Stanley and I didn't have to reach too far for donations to assist with Pfeiffer's final arrangements. Some donations were anonymous, others very sad over the loss of such a great man. I accepted the responsibility of his final resting place. He was cremated and the few thousand dollars left over after the expenses were given to his daughter. For the next year or

> so, Stanley and I spent a lot of time together. I loved your dad. We laughed at all the shenanigans that Pfeiffer, Stanley and myself got into.
>
> On a personal note: your old man as well as Pfeiffer were and will always be my mentors.

There are inconsistencies here, obviously. In my father's story, Pfeiffer is held captive for his monthly supply of morphine by his wife and others, who use it for themselves. In Abe's version, the robbery is a single event, and the perpetrator is left blank. Instead, he focuses on Pfeiffer's ex-wife (same person?) and daughter, who don't appear in my father's version at all. I asked him about these differences. About the morphine:

> There was a seedy looking guy who walked right in. No keys needed. Dad called him out on his statement (taking care of Pfeiffer). He was covered in feces and evidence of morphine patches lay around the floor. The room was disgusting. The guy said he didn't know what had happened here and had to leave. We found a business card with his Hospice caseworker's name. I called. She confirmed what dad already knew, that someone was stealing his pain patches. He was left there to die. He didn't even have the energy to dial a phone a few feet away from him.

And then about Pfeiffer's wife or ex-wife: "We called his wife and she met us at the hospice a few hours later with Steve's daughter. He was already gone. His wife looked typical of a junkie. No emotion. His daughter was maybe twelve or thirteen years old and visibly broken-hearted."

I can understand why Abe chose to leave that out the first time: the version we tell other people is the version that becomes true. What I remember now is the end of the conversation with my father outside the apartment building, after he got back from Buffalo. "You rescued him," I said, trying to make him—no, make myself—feel better. Less frightened. "Just like he tried to rescue you."

"I guess," he said, unusually reluctant to be soothed.

A nervous tremor ran up my back. "He was lucky to have a friend like you."

Voicemail

Now that he was back to practicing law, my father hired me to come in and listen to his voicemail. Three days per week, I would go to his home office, dig through the piles of dress shirts heaped on his desk, the stacks of shoes, the silk ties, find the phone, punch in the code, and listen.

On my first day, there were ninety-seven messages: court clerks telling him that he had missed a hearing; judges threatening him with contempt charges if he failed to appear; clients calling from the hallway outside the courtroom (*Stanley, where are you?*); prisoners calling from a pay phone in jail. The prisoners would leave three, four, five messages in a row, one right after another, reciting stories of false arrest and mistaken identity not even they seemed to believe. Still, they repeated them over and over like the scripts of a daydream. *Mr. Siegel, please call my mother. She'll tell you what really happened, and then you can tell the judge. He'll listen to you.*

Stanley, I'm in Rikers. You've got to visit me so I can explain.

Lawyer Siegel, I need to talk to you. When can I reach you? You're never there.

These clients were different from the old ones: they were assigned by the courts because they couldn't afford a private attorney, and the state paid their fees—very low fees. There were rambling complaints about asthma and diabetes and blood pressure, about unemployment and poverty. Just listening, my head started to hurt from the misery. I jotted down their names and court dates, and then I went downstairs to the McDonald's across the street, where my father was waiting for me.

Stepping inside that McDonald's was like walking into an urban wormhole outside time: homeless people with shopping carts; teenagers playing hooky; taxi drivers who looked as if they had worked the night shift in a trance and then forgotten to return the cab; children sitting next to their nannies, examining the toys from their Happy Meals; patients from the methadone clinic down the street, nodding out. The employees behind the counter attended the silver machinery as if they were manning the boiler room of an ocean liner headed somewhere distant and lonely.

He was at a table, sipping coffee with a contemplative expression. I sat down across from him, opened my notebook, and ran through my notes, the cases and court dates, the threats from judges, and then I told him about the prison calls. "Don't you ever listen to these?" I asked. "Some of them were pretty old."

He took another sip. "Why do you think I hired you?"

"I should be charging you a lot more," I said.

"You know it's bullshit, right? There is no new evidence."

I knew that. You didn't have to be a lawyer to recognize the illogic of their stories, the element of theater. They didn't expect you to believe it, exactly, but they couldn't not try, either. "There must be something you can do," I said. "Even just get them sentenced faster."

My father closed his eyes. "Nothing's going to help them." The truth was that he couldn't learn to love these new clients as he had once loved the old ones; he didn't want to be needed in that way anymore—maybe it was too frightening.

"Let's go fill out some vouchers," he said. He got up and went over to the drink station with its condiments and cups, and began filling his pockets with little blue packets of Equal, the artificial sweetener—grabbing big handfuls, unconcerned about who might be watching. Upstairs, in the apartment, he would make himself cups of instant coffee, mixing in the Equal with a look of great satisfaction. There seemed to be a particular sweetness to stolen sweetener.

Later, when he was in the hospital after his final collapse, one of the psychiatrists there would speculate that it was coffee and cigarettes, along with the amphetamines his psychoanalyst had prescribed him, that had been keeping him functioning so long through the early stages of dementia. But we didn't know that then. It never occurred to me that anything was wrong with him other than ordinary life—the thing that was wrong with all of us.

Here, he said. He took a handful of Equal and shoved it in my pocket.

HAIKU FOR MY FATHER

Sick on a journey—
in my dream staggering
over withered fields.

THIS IS THE LAST haiku ever written by the seventeenth-century Japanese poet Bashō Matsuo. He dictated it from his deathbed in a rented room over a florist's shop in the city of Osaka, in the autumn of 1694, too weak to use the writing brush himself. A few days later he was dead.

I stumbled across the poem for the first time soon after my father died, and it has fascinated me ever since. Just seventeen syllables in the original Japanese, it somehow manages to talk about the loneliness of individuality, the sorrow of ending, the yearning to travel onward—even if that journey can continue only in the imagination.

Does it seem as if I'm reading too much into a poem that is, after all, just a sentence long? It helps to know a bit about Bashō himself.

Bashō had spent the ten years before his death as a kind of wandering poet-priest, crisscrossing Japan on foot at a time when travel was dangerous—the roads little more than mud tracks through lonely countryside and wild mountains full of brigands. Dressed in the robes of a

Buddhist monk, he had walked hundreds of miles with a pack on his back to visit Buddhist temples and Shinto shrines, ruined castles, famous battlefields and places of unusual natural beauty, all of which became the subjects of his poetry. He did this to sharpen his sense of both the wonder and the brevity of all things, and to remind himself that life itself is nothing but a journey, a pilgrimage in which everything is always in flux. To experience the world in this way was a religious act for him, and the poetry he wrote a form of religious devotion.

He barely gave himself time to recover from his longest journey ever—a five-hundred-mile trip through rugged northern Japan—when he set out for Osaka in 1694. He probably knew it would kill him. Osaka was just forty miles from his home outside of Edo, and he was only fifty, but he was so physically broken from his years of wandering that he could walk only a few miles at a stretch and finally had to be carried. Once in Osaka, he came down with a fever, which he ignored until it worsened and he couldn't get up. Shivering in his quilts, he dictated the poem I translated above: *Tabi ni yande yume wa kareno o kakemeguru.*

The first time I read the poem, something in me resisted. The word *dream* felt unusually abstract, especially for Bashō, the most physical and specific of poets; it seemed to make the poem into a rather simplistic metaphor, in which life is a dream and the world a barren field. *Sure, I get it, but so what? Tell me something I don't already know.*

Then something happened, a kind of imaginative grace. I remembered that this was not simply a poem, a made-up thing, but the actual words of a dying man. I pictured Bashō lying in his quilts, too weak to sit up, gripped by a feverish hallucination in which, from a great height, he watched his dream-self doing what he could not do: stagger homeward.

Suddenly I had trouble holding back the sorrow he, too, must have felt, the sorrow he had, in fact, hidden inside the poem, a relic to outlive him. In the days that followed, I would be in the midst of my ordinary domestic life—making a peanut butter sandwich for my son, Jonah, or pushing my daughter, Maia, on the swing in the backyard—when out of nowhere I would think of the poem. Then my face would go numb, my eyes start to ache, and I would feel as if something were reaching up through my throat, trying to be born.

ONE DAY, OUT OF nowhere, my father began having trouble walking. Suddenly, getting to the newsstand on the corner to buy the paper became a major undertaking for him: one slow, wobbly step after another, separated by long pauses, as if he were trying to remember what came next. We were all baffled and frightened by the change—he more than anyone—and yet he refused to let anyone go for him. He wanted so desperately to keep to his usual routine.

"It's my back," he told me. "I've got to see a chiropractor." He had invited me out to eat sushi, but was now making a scene in the restaurant, lying on the floor and doing stretches next to our table. The waiter hovered, looking alarmed.

"Maybe do that later?" I asked, offering him a hand so he could hoist himself up.

He ignored me, raising his arms over his head, grimacing. "A good realignment is all I need."

My eyes narrowed. I had just lost my job: Prof. Park's Korean Studies Publication Project had burned up its entire endowment in a Korean stock market crash. Why couldn't we talk about *that*? Why was it always *him*? I remember riding the subway home afterward, full of self-pity. Back at home I called David, who was now a medical doctor doing a fellowship in spinal cord injuries at a hospital uptown. "Dad can barely walk," I told him.

"I've seen," he said.

"He says it's his back."

"He's somatizing." Medical jargon for channeling the emotions into bodily discomfort. Our father had been tending to one or another hard-to-pin-down ailment for years, trying to find a name for his confusion in life. The new name was *I can't walk*.

"He's driving me crazy," I said.

A few days later, I got a call from my mother, who told me that my father had fallen in the street and been taken to the emergency room in an ambulance. She had spoken to him and he sounded all right, but I needed to go get him. "I'm leaving now," I told her, full of guilt at having ever doubted him or the reality of his problem. I put on my shoes and ran to the elevator.

But as soon as I stepped outside, something shifted and I went into a kind of reverse panic. How was I supposed to rescue my father? What if I didn't do it right? The hospital was on the other side of town, but instead of hailing a cab I started to walk, and though I was in a rush, I stopped at a fruit stand and bought an apple and ate it down to the core standing right there. A part of me understood that everything would change forever as soon as I reached the ER, and I didn't want that to happen. I wanted everything to stay the same just a little while longer.

When I finally got to the emergency room, I found him on a bed in an alcove, dressed in one of those short backless robes that showed his legs, white and vulnerable. "Help me up," he said. He seemed to think I could take him home without talking to anyone first, and I would have done exactly that, would have snuck him out the door still in his backless gown and into a cab, if the doctor hadn't shown up just then with a clipboard in his hands.

"Mr. Siegel," asked the doctor, addressing my father, "do you know who the president is?"

"What's it matter?" asked my father, "they're all thieves."

"True, but which thief is it now?"

My father smiled wolfishly, as he used to in court when he had nothing to go on but sheer nerve. He mentioned how disillusioned with politics he'd become, and then brought up the unusually fine weather we'd been having. But when the doctor wouldn't go away, he looked cornered. "Okay, I'll go with Carter," he said, deflated.

The answer was Clinton.

My father turned to me, looking sad and a little guilty, as if he'd let us both down. Now everything was going to change. "Are you afraid?" he asked me, offering his hand.

It seemed like an odd thing to say, as if I were the one in the backless gown, not him, but I took the hand, grateful. "What's to be afraid of?" I asked, and then realized I was trembling.

Later, a neurologist would tell me that full-blown Alzheimer's disease often announces its arrival in a single dramatic collapse: *massive decompensation* was the term he used. He added that the illness had probably been progressing for a long time, a decade or more. It sounded like an accusation, and I bristled: I knew my father, and there had never been anything wrong with him, nothing we could see. If there had been, I would have done something.

Yet when I stopped to think about it, I realized that all the evidence had been out in the open for us to recognize if only we had wanted to. Shouldn't we have known something was wrong when he started sending profanity-laced letters to *The New York Times*? Or when he opened a package of lox spread in the supermarket, scooped some out with his finger, and then put the package back on the shelf? Or when he locked himself in the bathroom and couldn't get out? How about when his driving became so scary that Sean started chauffeuring him around town? And then there was the afternoon he spent wearing swim goggles around the house . . . Perrin called him The Situationist, after the French art movement that staged street happenings designed to disrupt bourgeois social norms. We had been great at explaining everything away with a joke.

So had he. When I told him that he had to buy the lox spread now, he laughed. "At these prices, snacks should be included."

It took me a while to put all that together. In the present moment, there was only the spectacle of my father in the hospital room to which he'd been moved. He lay in the bed as if drunk: incoherent, slurring his words, his eyes glassy and half closed. He didn't seem to know where he was. The next day, he was wide awake and talkative, but he sounded like an Ashbery poem, a mysterious flow of language outspeeding its meaning. I stood beside his bed, nodding as he talked on and on, wondering how we had gotten here from a bad back. "Dad," I interjected, "I've got to go home for a little while, but can I get you anything before I leave?"

He looked at me pleasantly. "Maybe just a blow job."

I nodded again. "Okay, I'll see you tomorrow."

The psych resident on his case, standing off in the corner, started to guffaw. He was dressed in a white shirt that looked as if it hadn't been changed in days, and he seemed half-mad with exhaustion.

In the days that followed, my father started getting out of bed and falling, so we hired an aide to stay with him and make sure he didn't wander and hurt himself. Honestly, he was probably trying to escape; he had moved into a new stage in which he feared his surroundings. The look in his eyes was horrible to see, a mixture of terror and rage, a kidnap victim's expression. He began screaming at the aide, pushed away a nurse who tried to take his blood pressure. "Don't you fucking put a hand on me!" he wailed, and both the fear and the violence in his voice reduced me to a child with no idea of what to do. When nobody from the family was present, the hospital put him in restraints, cuffing his hands to the bedframe. We objected to that, so they knocked him out with an antipsychotic drug instead; he slept for two days straight without opening his eyes; we couldn't even shake him awake. When we objected to *that*, they moved him to the psychiatric wing, where people wandered in their pajamas, weeping, and attendants who looked like NFL linebackers handed out little paper cups of pills.

One of those evenings, I was at home, getting ready to go back. I hated going but couldn't stay away: the hospital had come to seem like a dangerous place to leave my father alone. Jonah, who was two, asked me why I was leaving again; he wanted me to spend time with him. "I've got to go take care of Grandpa. He's sick."

"How sick?"

"Very sick."

He seemed to think about this. "You lift him up, Daddy. You lift him up, up, up." He raised his arms higher and higher into the air, stretching his frame. The idea was clear: I was to put my father on my shoulders, like I did for my son.

We switched hospitals and neurologists, fought with everybody, pushed for more and more tests, got used to being glared at by the staff whenever we walked in the door. The days went by, and our father seemed to come back to himself, though it was a weird new version of himself, with halting speech and that strange, shuffling walk, as if making his way across ice.

I remember taking him in his wheelchair to a cognitive therapy class in the building, led by two women who used a blackboard to guide the patients through three or four very simple crossword puzzles. One by one, the members of the class struggled to fill in the blanks: a three-letter word for motor vehicle, beginning with C; a two-letter word that means the opposite of *down*. After the last puzzle, one of the women asked if there were any questions. My father raised his hand in response. "I have a question," he said, sounding as if he were cross-examining a witness. "And I would like a straight answer."

"Yes, of course."

"I have been trying to find out what happened to me. What *is* happening to me." I could see him trying to put on his old face, the one he used in the courtroom with judges and juries. "But wherever I seek an answer, I come up against a wall."

"That must be frustrating for you," said the woman.

"It is. It is very frustrating, and I'm growing tired of it. I deserve an answer."

"What do you think has happened to you?"

A crack in his suave expression. He looked frightened. "I don't want to say."

"You don't want to say?"

His enormous brown eyes seemed to melt. "Yes, I don't want to say, because if I did, I'm afraid it would force me down a path I don't want to take." He began to cry, his chest heaving up and down, his bare forearms, thin and white, gripping the arms of his wheelchair. I shifted from foot to foot, not knowing what to do. We had, in fact, already settled on a diagnosis of Alzheimer's during a meeting in the neurologist's office a couple of days before. My father had sat listening, a vacant expression on his face.

We brought him home from the hospital, wheeling him into an apartment he didn't seem to remember. The disease moved quickly after that, quicker than it was supposed to. I'd read that Alzheimer's takes decades to play out, but within a couple of weeks, he'd lost the ability to walk. Moments later, he'd forgotten he'd lost it, clambering out of his wheelchair and collapsing to the floor. David, Sean, and I lifted him up and back into the wheelchair. "Dad, you have to stay in your wheelchair, okay? You can't get out," I told him.

"Okay, sure." He nodded earnestly.

"You understand? Don't try to get up."

"I'm not deaf."

I went off to the kitchen and came back to find him spread-eagle on the floor again. It was a kind of Abbott and Costello routine, played for horror instead of laughs. My mother finally seat-belted him in and he pulled at the belt, unable to figure out how to unlatch it, screeching profanities at us: *You mother fucking, cock sucking, shit eating* . . . The worst part of it wasn't the tirade, but how oddly impersonal it sounded, as if he were screaming at strangers. For the first time, I worried that he didn't know who I was.

Had he forgotten me? The question was too painful to ask, but I was aware that he didn't ever use my name, or ask anything about me, or register the distress I was feeling when I picked him up off the floor and put him back in his wheelchair. Maybe it was because his own distress was so much greater, or maybe it was because the guy who had taken my hand in the ER had been switched out for another identical but neurally damaged version of that person. I knew this, but nevertheless the thought that he had forgotten me felt like a threat aimed at the center of my own identity. It was a knife pointed at my chest, and he seemed to be the one holding that knife in his hand. I blamed him.

Nowadays, I never think about the year that followed. Not about the golden period, just a couple of weeks long, in which he would sit with the *Daily News* spread on the table in front of him, slowly deciphering a story about baseball. Not the day when the words in the paper finally became gibberish to him and he couldn't read anymore. Not the last time I saw him, near the end, when he was propped up in a bed in his home office, staring at the wall as if unaware of his surroundings. He did not seem to register my presence. He had given up eating, had long ago stopped talking, and his hands were curled in toward his chest, an effect of the brain damage. I never think of that moment, of how, though completely still, he looked like he was driving somewhere very fast.

LATELY, WHEN I RECALL Bashō's poem, I tend not to think about it so much as simply live inside of it, watching the scene from a great height, as if I were a bird. I see bare trees and empty fields, without a trace of human presence, except for a single lone figure, staggering over the furrows. The figure drifts to the right and then the left, falls to its knees, and then gets up again. It is the wandering poet-priest Bashō, so feverish he can barely walk and yet determined to keep going, to get home, even if that can happen only in the imaginative space of his poem, beyond the confines of his body and the limits of time.

And then I dip down for a closer look and see that the figure is not Bashō but my father, and that the dream, the wish for the safety of home, is my own.

The Heron

THE FOUR OF US stood back to admire our handiwork: eight spindly tomato plants tied to stakes pushed into the ground. With the kale and the peas to the left, and the carrots and basil to the right, the little corner of our backyard that we'd marked off for a garden was full. My wife and I hugged; the kids cheered.

We were transplants, just like those tomatoes. We had moved to North Carolina from New York City, where we'd lived in an apartment ten stories above the West Side Highway. Our backyard had been the dingy brown hall that led between the garbage chute and the elevator; that's where we ran our children on days it was too wet to get to the park.

And here we were now, standing in an earthly paradise, a little bewildered by this kind of happiness. It wasn't an unusually large backyard, no bigger than our neighbors', but it seemed vast. The air around us was busy with big fat bees and butterflies of a strange flittery green. An enormous, brawny pecan tree rose behind us, and droopy or bushy flowering things ran along the fence: camellias, azaleas, roses, lilies, lantana, wisteria, jasmine—we were still learning the names. In the center of it all rose a magnificent pine tree, taller than our house.

The next weeks were busy, but now and then I would kneel beside the tomato plants, amazed first by the hard green knobs that had sprouted among the leaves, and then by the way those knobs began to fill out and take on that familiar shape I knew from the supermarket, to grow red and soft. This might actually work, I thought, realizing for the first time that I hadn't expected it to, that I had assumed the plants would wither and my family and I would get in the car and speed back to New York, where life would resume its familiar, safe shape.

A part of me *wanted* to get in the car and step on the gas. Living close to the land had a worrisome side. My daughter had found a snake by the azalea bush and I had pulled everyone inside for a week, till I worked up the nerve to put on a pair of hip-waders, grab a baseball bat, and go searching for it.

And then there was the human element. The kindly old neighbor to our left had stopped me at the fence one morning to suggest that I cut down the pine tree. "Don't you see which way it's leaning? In a storm it'll fall down right smack on my garage." He gave me a sweet smile. "It's for your own protection, son. I'd be heartbroken if I had to sue you."

I looked at the tree, which was straight, so thick I couldn't get my arms around it, and wondered what the local etiquette was in this kind of situation. Not knowing, I fell back on the New York version. "Of course, I'll countersue."

"Son, you just lost the best neighbor you ever had."

Those were the last words he spoke to us. From then on he just glared across the fence, and when he wasn't there to glare, he left his hounds outside to bark.

I brooded about all this, of course, because all of it seemed to have some mysterious bearing on whether we would survive in this strange new land. Seated on the front porch one night, I was so busy brooding that I almost missed the possum heading into the backyard. It was fat and squat, with an elderly bald head, big shining eyes, and a dirty leer like a men's room flasher—the wet smile of a creature up to some great, illicit pleasure. He seemed to be panting with the effort of making his short legs go. I watched him disappear into the darkness, horrified.

I slept badly that night. The sound of the bullfrogs was deafening and the sheer darkness through our windows felt awful and wrong. Night in New York was full of light from streetlamps and office buildings, but this darkness was black enough to hide snakes and possums. I waited till dawn, stepped around the spider web, and went out to look at the garden. And that's when I saw that someone had taken a single juicy bite out of each and every one of our tomatoes. The sense of violation was terrible. They looked like human bites, and I knew instantly that it was our neighbor, exacting his revenge. I also knew what I was going to do about it: kill his dogs.

My wife trooped out with the kids to take a look. "It must be that possum," she said.

"Hey, look," said my son, pointing up at the pine tree.

A bird as big as a child was perched in one of the topmost branches. "A blue heron," I whispered, too awed to raise my voice. "Just like in the bird book." It had a long neck and hunched shoulders and a fiercely intelligent face reminiscent of my father. We watched as it took flight, heading to the creek beyond our yard. My wife and I hugged; the kids cheered.

NOTHING THAT WANTS TO RUN AWAY

When someone asks me why I'm a vegetarian, I usually bring up how the pig farms in our part of the state gather their waste in open cesspools the size of football fields, where it turns a weird shade of pink and then leaches into the groundwater. Or I talk about world hunger and how it takes fifteen pounds of grain to produce just a single pound of beef, on a planet that now holds over seven billion hungry people. Or I mention the old pair of pants I now fit into, or how much my cholesterol's improved, or the odd fact that animals seem to like me more.

But, really, it's all bullshit: I'm a vegetarian because of my father.

When I got the call that my father was dead, it was evening, and quiet. The children were asleep. It was my sister on the other end of the line, and she said something simple, on the order of, "Well, it's happened," and I said something oddly stilted and formal, like, "Yes, of course, I understand," as if I were talking to someone from the bank about an overdraft. My father was seventy-two and had been sick for a while with Alzheimer's, but somehow I'd never imagined this moment, never prepared for it.

I went upstairs and packed a bag—many pairs of socks, for some reason, but no shirt or underwear—and then I turned off the lights and climbed into bed, where I imagined that I could once again hear the rusty wheeze of my father's breathing, as if he were present in the room with me.

It's hard to describe now the weird sense I had of his lingering *thereness*. At the funeral in New York, I took one look at the plain pine box standing on sawhorses by the grave and knew with absolute certainty that it was too fragile to contain him. Back in North Carolina, a heron started visiting the pine tree in our backyard, and I took it as a sign. The bird was huge, with a great beak and beady eyes and long spindly legs, and he flew like an old man would, with a slow flapping of wings. Staring at him from the window, in the stillness of dawn, I began to cry, not out of sorrow but relief: my father was still with me.

At the same time, he obviously wasn't. I would wake up in the middle of the night in a panic, gasping for air, would get out of bed and sit in first my son's room, and then my daughter's, watching the gentle rise and fall of their chests as if looking for pointers on how to breathe. It wasn't sorrow, exactly, but something more angular and ugly—something a lot like fear. My father had died in old age of Alzheimer's disease, but to me it felt as if he had been murdered. Now that my eyes were open, I could see that, one day, I would be murdered, too—as would my two beautiful children, with their solemn, dreaming faces.

I carried that thought with me to the playground and the kindergarten pickup line, convinced that the beauty of the sunlight in the trees was nothing but a trick. I wanted to lodge a protest, to say, at least, "I disagree with death," but there was no way to do that without sounding like an insane person. And then one day, I looked at the hamburger I was eating for lunch and realized that it had once been alive, just like me, that it had been killed so I could eat it.

What if I didn't eat it? Wouldn't that mean a little less death in the world?

Then I grew timid and afraid, because I knew I didn't have the self-control to put the burger down. I *liked* hamburgers, and I was hungry. So I ignored the idea, feeling small and cowardly.

OF ALL THE THINGS we try to communicate, the hardest thing to explain may be why you love somebody. Once, when I was in my twenties and living in Brooklyn, I stopped by my parents' apartment in Manhattan and came across my father outside the building trying to reattach the driver's side mirror to his car. He was using duct tape. "Is that going to work?" I asked him.

"Probably not."

It was warm, and he was in a T-shirt, a chain around his neck with a bunch of medallions dangling from it: a Star of David, a St. Christopher carrying the baby Jesus, and a Buddha with the calmest face in the world. My father's great virtue was flexibility: he believed in luck and was willing to borrow anyone's.

That moment became my emblem of him: in his late fifties, trying to put his life back together with the cheapest tools available, through an act of loopy improvisation. He had met some reversals and was now meeting his clients in the McDonald's across the street, where he would fill his pockets full of blue packets of Equal to take home. I'd heard him on the phone, holding his nose and pretending to be his own secretary so he could claim to be out. "Does that fool anyone?" I'd asked, meaning, really, please don't do that, it breaks my heart.

"They're too shocked to say anything." He looked at me with a sort of wistful and bemused pity that he used to deflect my judgment. "Come on, let's bust Sean out of Care Bears."

Sean, my youngest brother, was four at the time. The three of us played hooky a lot in those days, Sean from Care Bears, my father from court, me from the novel that was really about him. We'd go to the park together, my father pushing the stroller as if he were chauffeuring a movie star. It took time to get anywhere because the two of them knew everyone in the neighborhood, had to stop and talk with the doormen and bodega guys and the man with the falafel stand and the woman who sold cigarettes in the little newsstand on the corner. My father gave money to every beggar we came across, dollars while he had them, and then coins, and then he'd be wiped out and I'd have to buy us all lunch. Nevertheless, when I fled my writing desk in Brooklyn, terrified by the blank page, it was to him I went. Somehow, when I sat with him in the sunlight in the park, some primitive voice inside of me, some remnant of childhood, said I would be all right.

A COUPLE OF YEARS passed after my father's death, and then something happened inside of me. Maybe I was simply old enough to feel how each winter, a little bit of the cold stays inside you, your gathering mortality. I realized that if I didn't give up meat soon, I never would, and I would die without having acknowledged how much I missed my father. I'll skip meat just this one day, I thought. I won't think beyond this one day. And so I left the meat on the plate and ate only the vegetables—and then did that the next day, too, and the next, and the next, single days like stepping-stones leading somewhere I couldn't see.

In the split of domestic chores, my wife, Karen, does most of the cooking. "I notice you're not eating any meat," she said to me one night, sounding a little aggrieved. Neither of us likes trouble when getting through our domestic chores. "Is there something wrong?"

I tried to phrase it gingerly. "I have an evolving sense of myself in relation to food."

"So, this is what, a diet?"

"I'm not giving it a label."

She looked at me as if I were causing a problem along the lines of our daughter's refusal to eat anything but chicken nuggets. "Let's make it simple, then—what *won't* you eat?"

I remembered how my father, in the middle stages of his illness, insisted on going to the newsstand on the corner for a copy of the *Times* each morning, even though he was losing the ability to walk. He would get there by staggering from lamppost to mailbox to parking meter, hanging on till he had the strength to move again. It looked like he was running from a murderer—and, of course, he was.

I said, "I don't eat anything that wants to run away."

It's been fourteen years since then, and I've never missed meat, never had cravings, never jumped in the car at two a.m. in a sweaty panic, looking for a Burger King. There are times when the ease of this change startles me anew, and I realize how much I used to worry that I would end up like my father, three hundred pounds and sucking taco mix out of the foil packet. Eating together was, after all, one of the things we did best: the steak for two at Peter Luger, followed by cheesecake at Junior's, or suckling pig in Chinatown, a movie, and then—why not?—pastrami sandwiches at Katz's. "You're an eater," he would say, grinning, "just like me."

But it turns out that I can love him without becoming him.

"SO YOU'RE A HUMANIAC now?" my brother David asked, when I told him I needed to order something vegetarian. We were in a Chinese restaurant on one of my visits to New York, soon after I'd stopped eating meat. Before I had a chance to pick a dish, he called over the waiter and began running up and down the menu: beef, pork, chicken, and squid. "Now that's a meal," he said.

The odd thing is that he's the animal lover, not me. I'm wary of dogs, and can't help but feel offended when they jump on me with their dirty paws. I'm shocked by the money people spend on their pets, and bored when they talk about them as if they were substitute children. I don't belong to PETA and haven't yet struggled with the ethical nuances of using animals in medical research. All I truly know at this point is that Porky Pig's right to scratch himself, dream, and generally be a confused idiot on the face of the earth is no different from my own: we're both alive, both made of flesh—things of the moment, full of yearning, doomed to end.

And yet, driving down the main drag where we live now, I sometimes look at the rows of fast-food restaurants, stretching for block after block, and I can see how the American hunger for meat interlaces with other problems: obesity, the automobile, suburban sprawl, billboards, and big-box stores, a constructed environment that features the parking lot as its primary aesthetic expression, a culture focused on truly insane levels of consumption and distraction. There is definitely something wrong with us, some kind of sickness of the mind, and I start to wonder if our blithe cruelty isn't a contributing factor.

Almost thirty-one million head of cattle were slaughtered in the U.S. in 2016 along with 118 million pigs, and more than eight *billion* chickens. Somewhere I've read the great Yiddish writer and vegetarian Isaac Bashevis Singer calling the eating of meat a Treblinka that never stops happening. I recoil from that statement even now, the way it connects the Holocaust to what most of us simply know as dinner. But then again, maybe I recoil because I secretly believe it's true: wasn't Treblinka just a slaughterhouse for people?

IN THE GLAMOROUS NEW Whole Foods market that recently opened near us, there's a huge flat-screen TV on the wall. It's in the meat section, and it plays a strangely beguiling video loop of pigs frolicking on an organic farm: rolling in the mud, scampering around a big open pen, what can only be called smiling into the camera. I remember the first time I stopped to watch, caught at first by the postmodern weirdness of the situation: a video of happy hogs mounted above a refrigerated case full of pork chops. Can nobody else see the problem here? I wondered. But a minute later I was wholly absorbed in the film itself, in the sheer spectacle of living things being alive in their peculiar way, snorting, rooting, chasing each other, so deeply immersed in the moment that there can be no thought of the future. It felt like somebody's home movies, and I stood there like an idiot as the loop repeated.

A Year in Taiwan

IF I HAD ONLY twenty seconds to describe the small Southern city in which I live, I'd tell you about our kids' soccer games, how the parents maneuvered their pickups and SUVs straight up to the edge of the field and watched through their windshields, engines and air-conditioning running, radios on—how isolating and sad that felt. Or I'd tell you about Market Street, the main thoroughfare we traveled to get to the soccer field, how it was lined with fast-food joints, each with a drive-through window, each with a vast cracked parking lot radiating the Southern heat, a dead zone.

I didn't want our kids to grow up thinking that this was how the world was supposed to look. I wanted them to know that this was a choice, a very particular American choice, so I took us all to Taiwan, where my wife and I got jobs at a university, teaching American studies. It was my first return to Asia in two decades; we were there for a year.

If I had only twenty seconds to describe Taiwan, I'd tell you about the campus cafeteria where we'd eat after Mandarin class, our heads still hot with strange new words for things we'd never thought of naming. It had sliding glass doors that were always open and the birds would fly about the long low room, twittering. I'd tell you about Harbor Road, the big avenue outside of campus, where nobody paid attention to the stoplight when it turned red. I'd tell you about the motor scooters, and how the scooter drivers wore surgical masks and raincoats to keep the exhaust fumes off their clothes and so looked like a million careening doctors rushing to the operating room. Sometimes there'd be a dog perched between their feet, sometimes a child standing in front of the handlebars, gripping the side-view mirrors for balance, sometimes a girlfriend on back, hugging the driver—a heartbreakingly profound sort of intimacy that everyone treated as invisible. There must have been couples that rode all night, just to touch in that way.

We lived on campus, in a ramshackle Japanese colonial house, exuding rot and charm: wood floors, sliding doors, big windows, swooping tile roof. There were geckos walking across the ceiling and frogs in the kitchen. Outside there were cobras in the tall grass, bats at dusk, cranes with long, elegant legs. The main walk through the university was lined with banyan trees, their branches looking as if they were dripping into the ground. Jonah and I would walk to the tennis courts and play in the dusk, the bats swooping down to catch the ball and then arcing away in the blue half-light. Afterward, we would stop by the basketball courts to watch the students play till it was so dark that watching became a form of listening.

The Taiwanese believe that you have ten different souls inside your body. Sometimes one may slip out, like a cat that's found the door left open. To get it back you need to stand at the crossroads and yell your name, over and over, till it returns to you. Once, unable to sleep, I stood in the darkness outside our house, listening to the immense rush of insect noise, the cicadas, frogs, lizards rustling in the bushes. I felt the wet heat on my skin, imagined the snakes moving in the underbrush. I closed my eyes and felt the place inside my chest where my missing soul should have fit. But I did not call it back. I decided to let it wander out in the world like another pair of eyes.

FRAGMENTS FROM A TAIWAN NOTEBOOK

A DAY OR TWO AFTER our arrival in Taiwan, my family and I stood at the edge of the narrow road just outside the college campus where we now lived, wondering how to cross the street. There was no traffic light, no crosswalk, no sidewalk, and no break in the traffic, which was made up almost entirely of motor scooters. Coming from America, land of the monster truck, a motor scooter sounds like a child's toy, but a torrent of them is actually pretty scary. We watched for a while, looking for a gap in the flow, lurching forward and then retreating. Finally, we lost heart and went home.

In the weeks that followed, we learned how to cross that street, zigging and zagging between scooters with the casual air of a Taiwanese college student out for bubble tea. We never really stopped to consider how out of character that was for us, anxious American suburbanites normally obsessed with rules and safety—tending to equate the two, really. It was as if we'd left our order-loving, non-jaywalking selves behind in America, along with our two overweight cats and Big Gulp cups.

Meanwhile, in our travels through the city, we were becoming connoisseurs of the sheer oddness of Taiwanese traffic. There were the hearses, of course, golden pagodas on wheels broadcasting Buddhist chants through loudspeakers, grand and a little bit eerie, like billboards for mortality. And there were the garbage trucks, playing their tinny version of "Für Elise" over and over again, announcing it was time to bring out the garbage. We once saw a truck with a jury-rigged platform high up atop the cab, a couple of men sitting up there for no apparent reason, nothing to hold on to. We saw a pickup truck with a table and chairs in the bed, two people seated on the chairs as if having tea at home. We regularly saw families of four jammed onto a single scooter, a baby held under the arm like a football. We saw scooters with dogs and cats and even, once, a parrot perched on the handlebars. We saw people using scooters to transport lawn mowers and stacks of large-bore sewer piping. Once, a scooter whizzed by with five propane tanks on back, lashed together. In any other country, that would qualify as a missile; in Taiwan, it was just a guy going home for dinner.

One of my Taiwanese students showed up for class covered in bloody bruises, which he'd bandaged for some inexplicable reason with clear packing tape.

"What happened to you?" I asked.

He giggled, embarrassed. "I tried to make a left turn."

Taiwanese driving habits were an obsessive subject of conversation among resident foreigners, who described with great relish the most outrageous things they'd seen: the left turn across four lanes of traffic; the truck driver steering with his knees while eating a bowl of noodles with chopsticks.

Don't drive if you can avoid it, they all said.

I have no intention of driving, I told them.

But if you do drive, don't stop short at a red light, because the guy behind you will expect you to go through and he'll smack you from behind.

I'm definitely not driving, I said.

The problem is they believe in fate. There's no need to use turn signals if you believe in fate.

It was meant as a joke, but the truth was that I'd been in cabs and buses where the driver kept a little shrine on the dashboard. One taxi, in particular, had smelled sweetly of sandalwood, and then I'd noticed a brown burn mark on the windshield where the incense burner touched the glass.

Of course, I ended up driving. I couldn't *not* drive, given all the intense feelings that clustered around it, all the thoughts about religion and culture and otherness, whether silly or serious, valid or invalid. And what I found, to my great surprise, was that I liked driving in Taiwan. Though I'd lived the last ten years in suburbia, land of the speed bump and the I BRAKE FOR SQUIRRELS bumper sticker, I'd grown up in New York City and originally learned to drive in the ferociously clogged streets of Manhattan, taught by a father who'd also run red lights and zoom up the breakdown lane when he thought he could get away with it. Fighting Taiwanese traffic thus felt oddly familiar, a return to patterns that, because of my father, lay buried deep inside me.

And then one night we were driving home on Harbor Road, Taichung's major avenue, when we heard a terrible boom up ahead, something between the man-made and the natural, a thunderclap and an explosion. Traffic slowed to a crawl, and when we finally crept past the trouble spot, I caught a glimpse of someone on the asphalt, lying on his stomach, very much as if he'd fallen asleep. A purposeful young man was standing beside him, waving traffic around. Other people stood at careful intervals, forming a neat perimeter around the rest of the scene, which included an overturned scooter and a helmet.

I do not want to write here about the dreamlike sadness of that scene. All I want to mention is that it struck me as very Taiwanese in its improvised orderliness—just as Taiwanese as the chaos of traffic. And it did not make me hesitant about continuing to drive, perhaps because driving had, by then, become a symbol of my sense of belonging. There was something deeply satisfying about lumbering down Harbor Road in my old Volvo, watching the scooters part ahead of me like little fish, as if we were in a Jacques Cousteau documentary. I might be a *waiguoren*, a foreigner, and my Mandarin might sound like the babble of a two-year-old, but I had my place in the ecosystem.

Indeed, as the months passed, I found myself driving more and more like a local. I didn't ever drive up the sidewalk, something I saw fairly frequently in Taichung, but I definitely did do whatever else might get me to my destination quickest, and I didn't bother to signal much while doing it. If you had seen my Volvo in action, you would have assumed there was no essential difference between its driver and the thousands of others out on the road.

Maybe that's a way of saying I was getting tired of being a *waiguoren*. One drizzly afternoon, idling by the curb of one of the city's biggest boulevards, with my eleven-year-old daughter in the back seat, I impulsively performed the maneuver that all the foreigners in the room had once identified as the great dividing line between East and West: I made a left turn across four lanes of traffic. It was, in fact, just the first part of a grand U-turn: afterward, we sat in the no-man's-land between the two sides of the boulevard, waiting for the light to turn green so we could make a second left and head back toward Harbor Road and home.

In retrospect, the best I can say for myself is that I felt ashamed. Yes, I had seen others perform the same stunt any number of times, but that didn't make it any less stupid. Such casual risk-taking felt inauthentic to me now, a form of pretension—perhaps because, deep down, I did not really believe in fate. I believed in traffic regulations.

I glanced into the rearview mirror, checking on my daughter in back, and then concentrated on the red light, willing it to change so I could get away and forget what I had just done. And then I heard a loud bang: someone on a motor scooter was smacking my passenger window with the flat of his hand. Hard.

I turned in my seat and tried to make him out through the tinted glass: in almost a year of navigating the streets of Taiwan, amid all the craziness and close encounters, I had never once witnessed an instance of direct, confrontational rudeness, let alone road rage. Drivers rarely even used their horns.

"He's got red hair!" said my daughter.

Leaning in, I could see it was true: he was a foreigner. Between blows to the window, he screamed at me in American English with all the fury of the self-righteous. "Four lanes of traffic! Four lanes of traffic!"

I was too frightened to roll down the window, too ashamed of myself to do more than mutter a defensive half-apology. "I'm sorry, everyone here does it," I said, knowing full well that he could not hear me over the radio and the air conditioning. "Stay awhile and you'll see."

The light changed, I drove away, and we were halfway down Harbor Road when I realized he probably couldn't see me through the tinted glass. He thought I was Taiwanese.

That confusion made me feel even more outside, rather than less. I didn't drive for a few days after that, wondering what had gone wrong with me, why my desire to belong was so reckless and stupid, why I couldn't find a better way. What would that better way look like? I couldn't visualize it.

Later that week, I drove the family downtown to Taichung Park, the oldest part of town, where the streets are all one lane and run in one direction. I took a left onto a side street and only then saw the construction blocking our way forward. I considered backing up but it looked like we might just be able to squeeze between the cement mixer and the parked cars if I pulled in our mirrors and my hands didn't shake. In any case, I could see in my rearview mirror that there was now a line behind us, so I had no choice. I started moving forward. And that's when I saw the blind man. He was in the middle of the narrow channel between the parked cars and the construction and he was walking straight toward us, tapping his cane. "You've got to lead him out of the way," I said to my wife.

I expected her to direct him to the side and then jump back into the car, but she misinterpreted and thought I meant lead him to safety. I watched the two of them walk past us, threading their way among the cars and the construction machinery. Somebody started to honk, and then others joined in, so I felt I had no choice but to drive on without her till I could find a place to pull over. But before shooting forward, I caught a glimpse of her in the rearview mirror, leading the blind man through traffic, one hand on his arm, whispering into his ear.

Stilt Walking

A WORKMAN COMES TO paint the living room ceiling after some repairs, and while he's working we have a long conversation in Mandarin. He seems to have a lot of problems with his boss—there's some profanity involved—and then he tells me a story about a relative in America who has either made a million bucks or come to a tragic end, I'm not sure which. As he talks, he sort of stilt-walks his ladder to the next spot, so he doesn't have to get down—a motion as deft and graceful as the cranes walking in the tall grass by the pond down the road. And I keep nodding and saying yes, yes, and hmm, and he keeps talking, and we are both perfectly happy.

MY MOTHER, MY WRITING STUDENT

On the first day of a weeklong creative writing workshop, I sit across from a group of serious-minded first-time novelists, people who have come to me, their teacher, to make their books better. I've just been going over the schedule, a series of craft talks, workshops, and one-on-one conferences. "Are there any questions?" I ask.

A hand goes up. It's the hand I've been dreading.

"Yes, Mom?"

Anyone who's ever taken a creative writing class knows how scary it is to show your work to a group of strangers. But what they may not know is how fragile the instructor can sometimes feel, too. Teaching writing seems so incredibly important to me that I can never completely overcome the suspicion that I'm slightly ridiculous, pretending to know something about the art of Faulkner and Proust.

And then add to the mix my mother, leaning forward in the seat in front of me, a determined and earnest expression on her face.

I look around at the other class members, all of whom are now gazing at me with a new sort of bemusement. "In the interest of full disclosure," I say, "Frances is my mother."

"I thought I saw a resemblance," says the woman to my left.

"It's the eyes," says another student. "You both look so serious."

"Robert's always favored my side," says my mother, looking pleased.

"Does this mean we have to go easy on her manuscript?" asks a guy in the corner, grinning.

"That's exactly what it means," I say—joking, and sort of not joking at the same time. I worry that my credibility is already draining away.

"Nonsense," says my mother, turning in her seat to face the others, barely suppressing a smile. "What good would that do me? I'm a writing student—just one who happened to give birth to the teacher."

MY MOTHER BEGAN WRITING after my father died: little fragments of things, a dream in which he spoke to her, an anecdote from their forty-year marriage. She wanted to recapture what was gone, to make him present again—or perhaps to acknowledge the strange fact that he was *still* present, even though he was nowhere to be seen. She would read these pieces to me when she came to visit in North Carolina, and I would listen with the bittersweet ache of recognition, hearing my father's voice, recognizing his quirks and mannerisms. My mother turned out to be good with words, an inspired sort of gossip, the kind who leans forward to lower her voice. "*Well*," she would begin, love, sorrow, amusement, and revenge mixing together.

I was happy that she had found writing, and yet a part of me was secretly annoyed, too. A small, childish voice inside of me said that writing was *my* thing, not hers. I had started writing twenty years earlier because I couldn't get a word in edgewise at home—about anything.

So, in some ways, I wanted her to go away and leave this most important part of me alone, even as I told her that my wife, Karen, and I would be teaching at a summer writing conference in Iowa that year, and that she should drive out with us and the kids and take some workshops. Even as I sent her the catalog. Even as I called her up to remind her about the registration date.

"I see you're teaching a novel workshop," she said. "It looks like just the thing I need."

I felt a surge of panic. "Wait, you can't take my class."

"Why not?"

I had imagined meeting for dinner at the end of a long day of workshops—separate workshops.

"Why not take the class on dialogue?" I asked. "You've always wanted to improve your dialogue."

"No, I don't like the guy's picture." She meant the teacher's faculty photo, which looked perfectly pleasant. "Besides, I need help getting started on my novel."

"What novel?"

"The one I'm starting."

"But, Mom," I said—and then realized that I didn't want to argue, because I wanted her with us. My kids were too young to remember their grandfather, and I wanted them to know their grandmother, which wasn't easy given that we lived seven hundred miles apart. She was seventy-five, and the only parent I had left. "Okay, sign up," I said.

AS THE WEEK PROGRESSED, the other students seemed quite amused by the situation, and not at all put off. They were a diverse group, including a woman from Belize who made her living as a traditional Mayan shaman, and a man who did something vaguely cloak-and-dagger in "computer security." From the standpoints of ancient herbal healing and cyber spying, what was so strange about a writing teacher who traveled with his mother in his class?

It helped that my mother was such a good student, listening carefully and making thoughtful comments. She didn't ask for special attention, or criticize my teaching, or otherwise try to diminish my authority. It all went beautifully, in fact, till I tried to talk her out of signing up for her student-teacher conference at the end of the week. "You're not like the others," I told her one night, after dinner. "If you have a question, you can ask me any time."

She drew herself up. "I paid my tuition just like everyone else, didn't I?"

"Yes, but—"

"Then fair is fair."

We met the next afternoon in the café that I had been using as a makeshift office. She sat down and took out her pad and pen. "So what do you think of my novel?" she asked, looking at me intently.

My mother's novel was an odd reading experience for me, and not just because it contained sex scenes. It was astonishingly well written, with a wonderful voice full of the verbal energy she brings to even the most ordinary conversation. But the main character was clearly an idealized version of herself, and whereas her previous pieces had been about recapturing the past with my father, this one seemed to experiment with an alternative life as a bohemian, and decidedly single, artist—a life that didn't include a husband or children.

My first impulse was to tell her that I couldn't help feeling a little hurt, given that she had effectively erased our whole family from the face of the earth just so that her imaginative alter ego could date a series of charismatic and very pretentious painters. But my next impulse was to stop and think.

It's always been a matter of faith for me that good writing begins with the ability to say what you want without worrying how others might react. Nothing worthwhile happens in writing without that basic expressive freedom. I'd worked many years to achieve that imaginative openness for myself, however tentative and fragile it still often felt. Did I want to refuse it to my mother?

"Yes, the novel," I said, stalling for time as the writing teacher and the son fought it out inside of me.

"You don't like it, do you?" she asked.

I looked at her across the little table, as she sat very straight and still, awaiting her writing teacher's verdict. Suddenly, I could see the emotional logic driving her novel: if she hadn't married my father, she wouldn't have had to suffer the pain of losing him. And I could understand how imagining that pain away might look like an attractive option right now.

"I do like it," I said to her. "I think it's got great potential."

"Really? You think it's good?"

"You have a terrific voice, but what you need now are more scenes.

The more you get your main character talking and doing things in scene, instead of explaining and describing in exposition, the more complex and interesting she's going to get. She'll start to grow in ways you can't plan or control."

I hadn't known I had advice to offer when I began talking, but there it was, almost in spite of my own intentions. And my mother seemed to understand it. She took some notes with a satisfied air, as if she could see her way forward.

We started the two-day drive back to North Carolina early the next morning. The car was crowded, and the kids were watching a movie on the DVD player, but my mother crouched over her notebook in her lap, writing with great determination. "Looks like you're on a streak," I said to her.

"It's *her*," she said, meaning her novel's protagonist, the freewheeling painter. "She's just so interested in everything. She never gives up."

Summer House

I HAD A LOT of trouble sleeping after my father died, but I didn't experience this as grief. I thought of it as *wakefulness*, an inability to fall sleep that felt oddly reassuring to me, like the presence of an old friend. My first memory of being unable to sleep is of a summer house at the beach with big windows and many doors, too many doors to allow rest—I remember five of them, brightly colored, red and blue. My father would work during the week and come out on weekends, and I think my mother was made afraid by his absence, which means that I was afraid, too. And I think I was genuinely afraid that my mother might disappear as well; she had that kind of flickering attention that created a sense of flickering connection. I would lie in bed, nervous but unclear on why, and stare at the shadow of the au pair, who had to sit there in the dark, poor girl, till I fell asleep. Watching her, the way she folded her hands in her lap, I would try to think about all the doors in the house and imagine them all locked, so nobody could get out.

THE DREAM BOOK

NOW THAT HE WAS gone, my mother wanted us to dream about our father. She called each one of us and asked if we had seen him in a dream yet, and was deeply disappointed when we admitted we had not. It was as if we were letting her down, failing at some important if obscure group effort to fast-track the mourning process. And yet she hadn't seen him either, and it had been four months since his death. "I wonder why he hasn't shown up yet," she mused. "Is he mad at me? Am I mad at him? We always had such trouble cooperating." She sounded annoyed, as if he had promised to drive her somewhere and was once again late to pick her up.

"I wouldn't read too much into it," I said.

"You know, your father would have been a great husband if only he had been less selfish."

"Mom, isn't it time to let go of that kind of thing?"

"Oh, it's never too late to understand people. That was one of his problems—he lived the unexamined life. So now I'm examining his life *for* him."

I don't know where she got the idea that we were supposed to dream about him. She told me that it was a commonly acknowledged part of what she called *the grief work*. "Everyone knows this," she said, sounding impatient. I didn't argue; it felt as if she'd earned the right to understand her loss any way she chose. After my father's diagnosis, she had taken early retirement in order care for him at home, giving up a job she loved to spend hours on the phone with the insurance company, to hire and fire home health aides, and to stand over them as they bathed him in the tub. She took him for walks, pushing his wheelchair around the block, and sat with him in the esplanade outside, in the winter sun, and fed him by hand while cooing endearments. "There you go," she had said, spooning applesauce into his mouth, because solid foods were becoming difficult for him to swallow. "Is that good? Yes, it's very good. I know it is. Very, very good." And then he had unexpectedly died within a year, much sooner than any of us had imagined. Now she had neither the job nor him, no distractions at all, nothing to keep herself from thinking about the past. I could feel her loneliness coming through the phone line, like the air that rushes through a subway tunnel before the train appears.

She named an old friend of his, also a lawyer. "You remember him? He called the other day. It turns out your father had dinner with him every Tuesday, for years. He never told me. If I asked where he was, he made something up. Why is that?"

My father had an ingrained and reflexive habit of evasion, an odd tendency to cover his tracks, even when those tracks were completely innocent, but I didn't want to think about that. Maybe because it made him feel blurry or shapeless when I wanted him to have clear, definite outlines. "Mom, I gotta go."

"You'll call me when you finally see him?" she asked.

"I don't normally remember my dreams," I said, hedging.

"But this kind of dream is different."

I hung up and phoned Perrin, not sure what I wanted to find out, feeling restless, vaguely worried. "Why did Dad hide things? You know, about where he was and what he was doing . . ."

"Honestly, I think he just wanted to eat without feeling guilty about it." Until secrecy became a habit that stretched to include everything.

"Compulsive overeating," I said.

"Yeah, basically."

And yet no one theory really covered everything, which is why we always went round and round, adopting one and then discarding it and picking up another. "Mom would tell me this story," I said. "About when they got married and she started to worry that he was a drug addict." I was a little boy when she first began repeating that tale. She always laid it out with a bemused air, as if it were a celebration of my father's childlike eccentricity and their warm, comically hapless union.

"I've wondered about that too sometimes."

"But he always made such a huge point about *not* using them," I said.

"It's hard to say what was really true," she said, growing quiet. "The one thing I never doubted was that he loved me."

We sat in silence for a moment. I had a sudden memory of being in the car with my father, parked on a street in Coney Island near the boardwalk, eating hot dogs from Nathan's. My clothes were damp from the rain. Rain pounded on the roof of the car, and the windshield was a sheet of water, impossible to see through. It felt as if we were under the ocean in a diving bell. What were we doing there? I couldn't remember, and it didn't matter. What lingered was the feeling of absolute peace.

I hung up and walked over to my desk, pulled a clean new notebook out of the drawer, and wrote *Dream Book* on the cover.

Since the funeral, I had been having a lot of trouble sleeping. I would spend nights counting the children's breaths, and then at dawn I would go to the window and look out at the backyard, where the blue heron had taken to sitting in the pine tree behind our house. The bird had mournful eyes, and it flew with great, slow flaps of its wings, its thin legs stretched out behind itself in a sort of tired Superman posture. It was my dad, just as he had been, slouchy and oddly dignified. I would stand at the window and cry in silence so as not to wake my wife.

But he wasn't just the heron. He was all over the place. I could feel him in the color of the sky at sunset, turbulent pinks and reds, low-hanging clouds. I had, in fact, seen him on the other side of the street just the day before, walking at a fast clip. I had crossed the street and followed him at a distance, but lost him around the park with its big cypress trees.

WEEKS PASSED AND I did not dream about my father. He was holding back, squirreling himself away for safekeeping as he so often had in real life. I called David to see if he'd seen him, but he sounded leery of our mother's plan and changed the subject, telling me he'd gotten our father's suits altered and was now wearing them to work. I knew those suits: browns that were almost plum, grays that were luminous, nearly blue. Pink pinstripes. "Dad always had great taste," David said. It was true: when he wasn't depressed and looking homeless, he walked the grungy marble hallways of the criminal court building like the star of a screwball comedy, jaunty and elegant.

"Do you want his shoes too?" I asked, meaning the dress shoes my mother had insisted I take home after the funeral. I'd had them almost six months and hadn't even tried them on. They were too beautiful to touch.

"Not my size," said David.

"Maybe you could get them stretched or something." The truth was that I wanted to get rid of them. Just having them in the house felt wrong.

He told me it wouldn't work, and the conversation petered out. Afterward, I went to the closet where the shoes resided like deposed kings and held one in my hand, breathing in the earthy richness of the leather, feeling its surprising softness. I had done this before, had thought of slipping one on for a moment, but could never bring myself to do it. My father's manic swings had been marvelous to watch, but I had identified with his depressions, and had therefore spent most of my life dressing in cast-offs and hand-me-downs. I put the shoe back with the others and grabbed a pair of old sneakers instead.

It was Sunday and there wouldn't be any kids in the park. My plan was to walk with Jonah to the coffee shop in the failing strip mall with the megachurch and buy him a piece of cake, just to get him out and expend a little energy—he was three years old, a whirlwind. But halfway there, we got sidetracked by the old military cemetery, which is to say that he suddenly veered off and darted inside the gate. I saw him running down a row of little white headstones, and, in a second, he was gone. I lost sight of him, which caused a moment of panic—that moment of terror when I could glimpse the world without him. And then I found him, and just like that, the fear was a residual tingling in my body.

"What are these?" he asked, pointing to a white stone marker.

"Gravestones," I said, still panting from the run. "When people die they don't need their bodies anymore, so we bury them here and mark the place with a stone."

His look was serious. "When people die, do they stop and get better, or are they dead forever?"

"Forever. They live in our memories. We think about them."

"Is Grandpa buried here?"

He had been angry when I didn't take him with me to the funeral in New York, so angry that when I got back he had ripped up the photograph of his grandfather I'd brought in my luggage. "No, Grandpa is buried in New York," I reminded him.

He nodded. "Do we bury their bones or their skin?"

"The whole body goes in a special box we call a coffin, and we bury it."

"And what do these say?" he asked, gesturing to the line of headstones.

"They say their names." I read the inscriptions out loud for him as we walked back toward the gate, the elaborate Southern names sounding exotic to my ears. All people who were once alive, like us.

"So when people die, we turn them into words," he said.

I THOUGHT ABOUT THAT idea at the mini-mall and the coffee shop and the walk back home and over the next few days of ordinary life, the domestic routine, till the phone rang and it was Perrin on the other end. "Did I tell you that I dreamed about Dad?" she asked.

"Tell me." I reached for the notebook on my desk and opened it to the first page, ready.

"I looked up and saw him standing in front of me," she said, "so we hugged. 'Dad, I love you,' I said. 'I love you, too,' he told me. He was smiling and seemed completely unaware of what had happened."

"That he was dead?"

"Yeah. We stood there together, feeling very happy, and then a little creature came walking up to us, maybe three feet tall. It was a sloth."

"A sloth?"

"You know, one of those cute animals with the long hair and the very long arms and the wise, sad smile? He was walking on two legs like a human, which I don't think they normally do, and he took Dad's hand and Dad smiled and said to me, 'Got to go, Sweetie,' and then they walked off together."

The sloth—about the size of a child, cute, gentle. I remembered watching my father walk off with my brother Sean when Sean was just a little boy, the two of them holding hands. I was in my mid-twenties back then, but the sight would make me achingly sad because I could never go home with them. I had my own life, such as it was.

I felt a furious need to interpret the dream, perhaps to keep our father from leaving with the sloth forever. "That sloth was you as a little girl," I told her. "Your unconscious mind was telling you that he's still alive, but in the past. The you of the past, the little girl, is with him there. The you of the present has to remain in the present, where he can't go."

"No," said Perrin. "It really was a sloth. I woke up crying. I knew that was the last time I'd ever see him."

My mother called a few days later. "I finally had a dream about your father," she said.

"Oh?" I went to my desk and got the notebook, opening to the page after Perrin's entry.

"He took me dancing. And he was such a fine dancer. We did a foxtrot up and down the length of the room. He looked wonderful, in a beautiful suit with a flower in his lapel."

"I didn't know he could dance," I said.

"He couldn't. His feet were like two bowling balls. But he can now."

At dusk, I went to the window and saw the heron there in the pine tree. He looked fierce and thoughtful, and we shared a moment of loneliness together. Later, I fell asleep and had the first dream I could remember in a very long time. It was one of those dreams in which there are no people and nothing happens: just a view of what seemed to be a block in our small city, downtown by the river. I half-recognized the old red brick buildings, the cracked sidewalk, the cobblestone paving. What was odd was the sky, pale and almost lemony, stretching on and on without end.

I don't always feel that good about the place we live, but in the dream the feeling was deeply good, a form of love. My dream-self instantly understood the significance of what it was seeing: my father was here, and the thing I most feared in life, that something would hurt my children, that I would fail to protect them—that would never happen. Instead, the world would rise beneath me and carry me up, like an ocean swell, and it would give me the strength to be their dad, and we would be happy.

I had slept much later than usual; one glance out the window and I could see that the heron was gone for the day, the pine tree empty. I got up and got dressed, and then went to the closet and pulled out a pair of my father's shoes: oxblood, cap-toed, with monk straps instead of laces. I put them on and noticed how different it felt to stand in them—firmer, taller. I was going to find that street downtown, the one that almost looked like the dream. Then I opened the door and stepped outside.

ACKNOWLEDGMENTS

DEEPEST THANKS TO MY beloved wife, Karen Bender, who read and commented with insight and kindness; to my children, Jonah and Maia, who reminded me that art is a form of play; to my parents, Stanley and Frances, and to my siblings, David, Perrin, and Sean—my fellow travelers. On the literary side, thanks to my marvelous agent Geri Thoma, to the intrepid Andrea Morrison, and to Dan Smetanka, editor nonpareil. Finally, appreciation to Abe Dickoff for his help with "Friends," and to the mysterious author of the blog *A Funny Thing Happened on the Way to the Grave*, whoever he may be.

A number of the essays in this volume first appeared in magazines and anthologies, though sometimes in different form: "Criminals" first appeared in *The Paris Review*; "Gourmets" first appeared in *Tin House* and was subsequently reprinted in *Utne Reader*; "Unreliable Tour Guide" first appeared in *Ploughshares*; "Sean" first appeared in *The Harvard Review* and was subsequently reprinted in *Freud's Blind Spot: 23 Original Essays on Cherished, Estranged, Lost, Hurtful, Hopeful, Complicated Siblings* and *The Pushcart Prize Anthology XXXVI: Best of the Small Presses*; "Haiku for My Father" first appeared in *The Los Angeles Times*; "The Heron" first appeared as "Ode to My Backyard" in *The Oxford American* and was subsequently reprinted in *27 Views of Wilmington: The Port City in Prose and Poetry*; "Nothing That Wants to Run Away" first appeared in *The Harvard Review*; and "My Mother, My Writing Student" first appeared in *The New York Times*. Gratitude to these publications and to the wonderful editors—Lorin Stein, Michelle Wildgen, Elisa Albert, David Ulin, Bill Henderson, and Christina Thompson in particular—who helped me make sense of my experience on the page.

Author photograph by Jonah Siegel

ROBERT ANTHONY SIEGEL is the author of two novels, *All the Money in the World* and *All Will Be Revealed*. His work has appeared in *The New York Times, Los Angeles Times, Smithsonian, The Paris Review, Oxford American*, and *Tin House*, among other venues. Siegel has been a Fulbright Scholar at Tunghai University in Taiwan and a Monbukagakusho Fellow at the University of Tokyo in Japan. Other awards include O. Henry and Pushcart Prizes and fellowships from the Fine Arts Work Center and the Copernicus Society of America. Find more at robertanthonysiegel.com.

Printed in the United States
by Baker & Taylor Publisher Services